TOP-RATED
AZALEAS and RHODODENDRONS
AND HOW TO USE THEM IN YOUR GARDEN

This book was produced for Western Publishing Company, Inc., by the staff of Horticultural Associates, Inc., in cooperation with Amfac® Garden Products.

Executive Producer: Richard Ray
Contributing Authors: Alvin Horton, Michael MacCaskey
Consultants: Fred Galle, Past President American Rhododendron Society, Pine Mountain, GA; Carl A. Totemeier, Jr., Old Westbury Gardens, Long Island, NY.
Photography: Michael Landis
Art Director: Richard Baker
Book Design: Judith Hemmerich
Associate Editor: Lance Walheim
Research Editor: Randy Peterson
Copy Editors: Greg Boucher, Miriam Boucher
Production Editor: Kathleen Parker
Book Production: Lingke Moeis
Illustrations: Charles Hoeppner, Roy Jones
Typography: Linda Encinas
Additional Photography: William Aplin, Susan A. Roth
Cover Photo: Michael Landis
Acknowledgements: Ed Egan, Editor, American Rhododendron Society, Tigard, OR; Fran Egan, Secretary, American Rhododendron Society, Tigard, OR; Green Bros. Landscaping, Inc., Smyrna, GA; Dr. H.G. Hedges, Secretary-Treasurer, Canadian Rhododendron Society, Ontario, Canada; Longue Vue Gardens, New Orleans, LA; Nuccio's Nursery, Altadena, CA; Dr. Harold Pellett, University of Minnesota Landscape Arboretum, Chaska, MN; Planting Fields Arboretum, Oyster Bay, NY; Robert L. Ticknor, Past President American Rhododendron Society, Canby, OR.

For Western Publishing Company, Inc.:
Editorial Director: Jonathan P. Latimer
Senior Editor: Susan A. Roth
Copy Editor: Karen Stray Nolting

Golden Press • New York
Western Publishing Company, Inc.
Racine, Wisconsin

D1397980

Top-Rated Azaleas and Rhododendrons

Springtime commences in this country in the Deep South and the far West about St. Valentine's Day, and slowly advances northward until by Memorial Day the entire continent appears to be in full bloom. Everywhere, flowering trees and shrubs fill the landscape with masses of welcome color, finalizing the transformation from winter into spring. Throughout most of the United States azaleas are the heralds of spring.

When azaleas are in bloom, their delicate flowers appear so profusely that they entirely blanket the plants with color, completely obscuring the foliage and branches. Their blooms come in such an array of colors and forms that it staggers the imagination. In old Southern gardens, where azaleas are synonymous with spring, enormous, spreading plants with layers of branches and masses of flowers may be as old as a hundred years. Estate and public gardens that feature these impressive plants attract visitors from around the world. The peak of their blooming season is celebrated by festivals in many of the old Southern cities, such as Charleston, South Carolina; Wilmington, North Carolina; and Savannah, Georgia.

Rhododendrons, close relatives of azaleas and generally more cold hardy, are just as awe-inspiring. Usually blooming later in spring, they are admired for their large bouquet-like clusters of flowers, called trusses, that crown the branch tips. Colorful azaleas and rhododendrons are planted to beautify

At left: Azaleas are in their glory planted in a woodland setting growing under the dappled shade of high-branched trees.

'Gibraltar' (Knap Hill/Exbury Hybrid)

'Sappho' rhododendron

'Rosebud' (Gable Hybrid)

Knap Hill/Exbury Hybrid azalea

Pontic azalea (R. luteum)

'Snow' (Kurume Hybrid)

Knap Hill/Exbury Hybrid azalea

home landscapes throughout most of the country and rank high as all-time garden favorites.

No other flowering shrub—not even roses—creates the seasonal splendor and year-round appeal that azaleas and rhododendrons do. There are azaleas and rhododendrons to suit every taste and almost every climate, over 10,000 named varieties. So many in fact that some avid gardeners specialize in collecting azaleas and rhododendrons. But you don't have to be a plant collector to enjoy these very special shrubs—they are easy to grow once you understand how to provide for their particular needs.

Top-Rated Azaleas and Rhododendrons is designed to help you select the azaleas and rhododendrons best-suited to your needs and to ensure your success in growing them. The 200 species and varieties described here were specially chosen as being top-rated plants. A group of experienced gardeners and professional horticulturists from throughout the United States and Canada selected these plants from the thousands that are available. Their choice was based on beauty, versatility, cold hardiness, durability, availability, and special considerations such as late season of bloom or unusual flower color.

Their rhododendron choices also take into consideration ratings made by the American Rhododendron Society, a group of azalea and rhododendron hobbiests and professionals. The society's ratings represent years of testing, often beginning well before a variety is commercially available. So it's no coincidence that top-rated azaleas and rhododendrons are the most reliable, attractive, and popular ones. But since a variety top-rated for Delaware is not necessarily top-rated for Oregon, regional recommendations are given for all selected rhododendron varieties and species; and for all major azalea hybrid groups and species.

A HISTORY ALL THEIR OWN

Azaleas and rhododendrons are native to moist woodlands and forests of North America, Europe, and Asia. Scores of rhododendron species grace the forests of the eastern Himalayas where the monsoon rains keep the soil and air moist, and the steep slopes provide for excellent drainage. Abundant also in Southeast Asia and Malaysia, rhododendrons are mostly understory trees and shrubs, enjoying the filtered sunlight that passes through the open network of overhead foliage. Several rhododendron species are native to the Appalachian Mountains.

Azaleas are found growing wild mostly in the mountain forests of Eastern Asia and North America. North America has an impressive offering of native azaleas, and many of these are graceful, colorful plants that are superb in many home landscape situations.

Compared to the rose, whose cultivation dates back to the beginning of history, azaleas and rhododendrons are recent arrivals to cultivated gardens. Though valued in the Orient for centuries, azaleas and rhododendrons were first discovered by Western gardeners in the 18th Century. At that time, avid English plant collectors explored and collected new and exotic plants from around the world.

Imported from Asia Minor, the golden-flowered and spicely-fragrant pontic azalea, *R. luteum*, was being grown in England by the time of the American Revolution. By the end of the 18th Century, many native American azaleas, including the yellow-flowered flame azalea, *R. calendulaceum*, and the pink-flowered swamp azalea, *R. viscosum*, were cultivated in Europe. Also, many new azalea species and natural hybrids had arrived from the Orient.

From the Appalachian Mountains four native American rhododendrons came to English gardens by the mid-1700's. These included the catawba rhododendron, *R. catawbiense*, with its masses of pink or lavender blossoms, and the rosebay rhododendron, *R. maximum*, a massive plant bearing rose or purplish-pink flowers in late June.

During the 19th Century, scores of azaleas and rhododendrons arrived in Europe from Asia and America. All of these American and Asian rhododendrons and azaleas were eagerly embraced by English, Belgian, Dutch, and French horticulturists, who crossed and interbred them in attempts to create even more spectacular plants.

The heyday of plant exploration was during the mid-1800's. During that time many daring explorers and collectors ventured into China and Japan, areas where few Westerners had ever set foot. In the mid-1800's, Dr. Joseph Hooker, son of the first director of Kew Gardens in London and ultimately his successor, trekked in the Himalayas and returned to England with more than 40 new species of rhododendrons. In 1843, Scottish plant collector Robert Fortune set out on a plant-hunting expedition in China. He discovered only a few azaleas and rhododendrons, but one of them, *R. fortunei,* has contributed its huge, fragrant, rosy-lilac blossoms to countless beautiful hybrid rhododendrons.

Perhaps the most famous plant explorer was Ernest H. Wilson, who, in the employ of an English nursery, made four journeys to China during the early part of this century in search of new and exotic plants. His exploits earned him the nickname of "Chinese" Wilson. From the high altitudes of southern and southwestern China, he introduced more than 400 new species of azaleas and rhododendrons. He found the elevation of 11,000 feet offered the most diversity, though he collected rhododendrons from even as high as 15,000 feet.

Explorer, plant collector, and author, Frank Kingdon-Ward, spent a half-century searching regions such as Assam, Burma, Tibet, and western China for rhododendrons. George Forrest, a Scottish plant collector who made seven trips to western China, was perhaps the most daring of all the explorers, risking his life to collect plants. He explored the interiors of China and Tibet by learning local languages and employing local people as guides and bearers. Somehow, he managed to survive warfare, malaria, and other tropical ills, as well as the ordinary rigors of mountain climbing. Many of Forrest's introduced species are important parents of today's popular hybrids.

During a span of two centuries, English plant explorers introduced hundreds of Asian and American azaleas and rhododendrons—both evergreen and deciduous species—to Europe. As Japan slowly became open to Western trade, hybrids created by Japanese gardeners were offered to the Western world as well, and their traits were drawn upon in the creation of newer hybrids. A fervor of plant breeding that began in Europe in the 1700's and that is still going on today is responsible for thousands of named hybrids and varieties.

HYBRIDS TODAY

Today the thousands of named varieties of azaleas and rhododendrons in existence offer a confusing array of plants to gardeners. Azaleas especially seem a confusing lot. There are deciduous kinds and evergreen kinds, and the named varieties fall into many hybrid groups. Rhododendron hybrids are perhaps less confusing because they fall into no hybrid groups, but this lack of organization provides no guidance in selecting from the thousands of varieties.

The first azalea species available to plant breeders were deciduous kinds. They were hybridized to create new color and fragrance combinations. When evergreen azaleas from the Orient became available, these were crossed with the deciduous kinds in an attempt to increase the color range and cold hardiness of the evergreen azaleas.

Once only plants for southern American gardens, today evergreen azaleas are grown as far north as Boston, thanks to the dedication of several hybridizers. The aim in azalea breeding is toward creating ever more cold hardy evergreen azaleas that can retain their foliage in the cold northern climates. And though deciduous azaleas come in the full spectrum of colors including yellow, red, and clear orange, the evergreen azaleas offer only an assortment of shades of pink, purple, red, and white.

THE GENUS RHODODENDRON

In 1753 when the famous biologist Linnaeus published his classification of all the plants and animals in the world, he had classified azaleas and rhododendrons in two separate genera—the genus *Azalea* and the genus *Rhododendron*. At that time he had seen only a few species, and those were from the New World. Today botanists recognize that these plants, though they appear quite different at first glance, have many similarities. They now are both grouped into a single huge genus, the genus *Rhododendron*.

Botanists look at these plants and see that they have the same kind of floral structure, pollen, and seeds. They all cross freely with each other and are therefore closely related. Modern plant classification places azaleas and rhododendrons in the same genus. Some botanists divide the genus into 43 series with azaleas making up one series. Other botanists divide the genus into 8 subgenera, with deciduous azaleas making up one subgenus and evergreen azalea another subgenus.

Gardeners, however, continue to think of them as separate kinds of plants. They think of azaleas as low plants covered with masses of flowers in spring and fine-textured evergreen or deciduous leaves. To a gardener, a rhododendron is a large plant with whorls of big evergreen leaves and distinct clusters of flowers.

Because gardeners continue to think of azaleas and rhododendrons as different kinds of plants, many nurseries label azaleas with the out-of-date genus name *Azalea*. For instance, the pink-flowered royal azalea, *Rhododendron schlippenbachii,* is often labelled *Azalea schlippenbachii.*

Using Azaleas and Rhododendrons in Your Garden

There are no hard-and-fast rules when it comes to landscaping—taste is an individual matter—but most home gardeners find that following some general guidelines can help in creating an attractive, functional landscape. Success in landscaping depends upon selecting plants that serve a particular use, that are enjoyable to look at, and that can adapt to the conditions of their planting site.

Azaleas and rhododendrons are among the most beautiful and useful ornamental plants. To show them off to best advantage, it helps if you understand just what makes them so lovely and what makes them different from each other. Keeping in mind their shape, texture, and color throughout the year, you will be able to effectively situate them and combine them with other plants.

SEEING AZALEAS AND RHODODENDRONS

It goes without saying that these are spectacular plants, but just what do you *see* when you look at these shrubs? Everyone admires the beautiful splashes of color they create in spring and early summer, but if you really study them, you'll see that each azalea and rhododendron has an individual character that is best taken into account when deciding what to plant and where to plant it.

At left: 'Hinodegiri' (Kurume Hybrid) is attractive year-round, making it an excellent choice for use in shrub borders or foundation plantings.

'Nova Zembla' rhododendron

'Toucan' (Knap Hill/Exbury Hybrid)

'Herbert' (Kaempferi Hybrid)

Knap Hill/Exbury Hybrid azalea

'Gumpo White' (Satsuki/Macrantha Hybrid) is effectively backdropped by red Japanese maple (*Acer palmatum* 'Dissectum').

Plantings of color-coordinated azaleas create dramatic visual impact.

'Purple Gem' is a dwarf rhododendron useful in small-scale gardens.

EVERGREEN AZALEAS

When in bloom, a well-grown evergreen azalea is blanketed with brightly colored blossoms and hardly a leaf is visible. Even a single large shrub creates a dramatic impact for the two weeks it's in flower. Planted en masse, azaleas are, quite simply, boisterous. Though some kinds have small, dainty flowers and others have large, showy flowers, the sheer abundance of blossoms overrides any textural impact the size of the flowers might create. A blooming azalea is anything but subtle.

Out of bloom, evergreen azaleas return to their quiet, elegant character. Their leaves are generally fine-textured, ranging in size from 1/2 to 4 inches long. The more cold hardy kinds, such as the Gable Hybrids, have the smallest leaves. Southern and Belgian Indicas offer larger, more lush-looking foliage. In fall and winter, foliage may take on beautiful glossy reddish, purplish, or bronze hues. This is especially true of the kinds with deep-colored flowers. White-flowered kinds have dark green foliage in winter.

Different varieties retain varying amounts of foliage during winter. Generally, plants near their limit of cold hardiness lose most of their inner leaves, keeping only a whorl or two of leaves near the branch tips. Azaleas that have strong evergreen characteristics make the best plants for foundation plantings and privacy hedges.

Evergreen azaleas can have a variety of shapes. Some are tall and wide, others are low and spreading. Branches may be dense and random, or arranged in distinct layers. It's best to choose a plant whose size and shape fits in with its landscape situation. Tall wide plants make better screening hedges, while low, spreading ones are better for foundation plantings.

Because evergreen azaleas are fine-textured and dense and display such a bold show of color, they are best in formal kinds of landscape situations. They make excellent foundation plants, and are perfect for shrubbery borders on the edge of a lawn, either mixed with other shrubs or planted in groups. They also make effective hedges.

Azaleas have been significant plants in Oriental gardens for centuries, pruned into elegant bonsai shapes, or pruned to accentuate their layered branches. At one time during the history of Oriental gardening, azaleas were not allowed to flower. They were kept pruned into artistic shapes and admired for their foliage and branch structure.

DECIDUOUS AZALEAS

Flowers of deciduous azaleas usually appear in large clusters at branch tips. Though flower size can be large and clusters can contain as many as 15 or more flowers, especially in the Knap Hill/Exbury Hybrids, the floral show is more subtle than with the evergreen azaleas. This is because the bold-textured flower clusters are not massed together as they are with the evergreen azaleas, and shrubs are looser and more open.

Most deciduous azaleas have tall, vase shapes made up of many upright stems. They are loose and open, giving a light airy feeling. When bare of leaves in winter, they have an especially delicate texture due to their slender, upright branches. The light touch is not lost when plants are in bloom, because flowers usually appear before the new leaves emerge, or if foliage is present, it is sparse.

Summer foliage does not obscure the branch structure and the shrubs maintain their graceful character. Leaves measure four or five inches long and are oval and pointed. They are bright green and frequently change to beautiful reds, oranges, and golds in fall before dropping, creating a second season of color.

The nature of their flowers, foliage, and branch structure gives deciduous azaleas a more informal character than evergreen azaleas. Because they are so open, they make poor foundation plants, except against rustic or modern-style houses with wood siding right down to the ground. They are best grouped in a shrubbery border, with a fence or other dense shrubs as a backdrop, or scattered in a woodland setting. They also make effective specimen plants beside a pond or in an Oriental garden.

SPECIES AZALEAS

These lovely, delicate-flowered plants have many things in common with the deciduous hybrids. They are usually airy shrubs that bloom before foliage emerges in spring. Their clusters of blossoms are frequently made up of funnel-shaped flowers whose long, curving stamens extend beyond the petals.

Most species have a graceful beauty that is best shown off in a natural woodland setting or a wildflower garden. Though their color impact in spring and fall is excellent, species azaleas do not blend well with evergreen azaleas. The explosion of color of the evergreen hybrids overpowers the exquisite grace of their wild cousins.

RHODODENDRONS

Many rhododendrons, especially old-time ones, are large plants with big, leathery leaves and balls of flowers at the branch tips. Such plants have a bold texture that commands attention. Large rhododendrons need plenty of growing room, but they also need spacious quarters so their texture doesn't become oppressive. Newer hybrids feature shrubs with more compact growth and smaller leaves, though flower cluster size usually remains the same. These plants are more suitable for small landscapes. Dwarf shrubs offer a medium texture and compact size that is useful in many gardens.

The big rhododendrons are excellent screening shrubs planted as a hedge on a large property or in the background of a shrubbery border. Their large, dense evergreen foliage blocks views and viewers year-round, and their stunning

Azaleas and rhododendrons have unlimited landscape uses in regions where their growth requirements can be met.

Pontic azalea, from Asia, *(R. luteum)* produces very fragrant yellow-orange blooms in midseason.

9

Azaleas and rhododendrons appear to best advantage in naturalized settings that echo their native growing environment, as shown above and below.

'Redwing' (Rutherfordiana Hybrid), bears masses of brilliant red flowers in midseason; has attractive foliage year-round.

clusters of speckled flowers provide dramatic displays. They also look at home planted in groups or singly under trees in woodland settings.

Though sometimes planted as foundation shrubs, large-growing rhododendrons grow too big too fast to be good along most houses. They will quickly block windows and crowd other shrubs. For foundation plantings, try compact or dwarf rhododendrons. Their coarse foliage looks best against wood shingles or stucco, and may look too busy when set off in quantity against bricks or stone.

DESIGN BASICS

The visual impact a plant makes depends upon its size and shape, the texture and color of its flowers, and the texture and color of its foliage. Plants are not static, and these attributes change throughout the growing season. For instance, deciduous azaleas have a medium texture during the summer when in full foliage, but when leafless in winter, their bare twigs are fine-textured. Skillful garden designers consider all these aspects when they select and locate shrubs.

Texture: Fine-textured plants are more restful to look at. When seen from a distance they appear smaller and farther away than they really are. When used in small or enclosed areas they make the space seem larger. Bold-textured plants have the opposite effect. When viewed from a distance they appear closer and larger than they really are. Planted in quantity in an enclosed space, they may seem too busy and overpowering.

Fine textures and bold textures can be combined to good effect, the contrasting textures creating visual excitement. Many garden designers group fine-textured plants at one end of the garden and bold-textured ones at the other end, so there is a visual progression from fine to bold textures. They also use larger groups of fine-textured plants, progressing toward smaller

groups of bold-textured plants. This keeps the visual effect from becoming too busy.

If you want the area to seem larger, plant the fine-textured azaleas in the distance and the bold-textured rhododendrons nearby. Do just the reverse if you want a large area to seem more intimate.

It's usually better not to mix deciduous and evergreen shrubs in a haphazard manner. Though in the summer they may have the same texture, in winter the deciduous ones will be fine-textured and appear weak mixed in with the evergreen shrubs. Plant the deciduous ones in groups among, and in front of, evergreen kinds.

Color: Considered alone, almost any flower has a beautiful color. But that beautiful color has to look good with the rest of the colors in the landscape. When choosing azaleas and rhododendrons, you'll be choosing from a full spectrum of colors including every hue and shade imaginable. When set side-by-side, many of these otherwise attractive colors will clash. Selecting plants when they are in bloom may help you keep color mistakes to a minimum.

Some azalea fanciers plan a border of azaleas around a color scheme. The pure pinks, purples, and magenta-reds are grouped together and separated from the warmer corals, oranges, and orange-reds by groups of white azaleas, or by other kinds of shrubs that won't be in bloom at the same time.

It is also a good idea to select shrubs that bloom at different times of the season. The flowering season of all the top-rated azaleas and rhododendrons included in this book is given in their descriptive entries. Choose a balance of early, mid, and late season shrubs so you will have a long, beautiful color display. You may wish to group the plants according to season so different parts of the garden are in bloom during different times. This gives the best show and avoids a polka dot look.

Many gardeners plant several shrubs of the same color together. This gives a more pleasing effect than a hodgepodge of random colors with each vying for attention.

When choosing flower colors, be sure to think about the colors already in the landscape. In a foundation planting, the flowers will be set off against the house. Magenta-red azaleas and rhododendrons look dull and dark against red brick, but are stunning against white clapboard. Other spring-flowering shrubs and trees will be in bloom at the same time and their blossoms should harmonize and complement one another. Favorite combinations are: pink azaleas and white dogwood; magenta azaleas and white spiraea; and purple rhododendrons and pink mountain laurel. Plant white azaleas with yellow forsythia and white rhododendrons with golden-chain tree for an elegant yellow-and-white garden.

Size and Shape: Little plants become big plants, rhododendrons and azaleas not excepted. Some grow more slowly than others and of course they ultimately reach different heights depending upon the variety. The temptation is always to plant new shrubs close together because they look best that way. But they only look good for a few years, then they become crowded and overgrown-looking.

Plan ahead and consider a plant's mature height and spread when you plant it. Put large-growing plants where there will be room for them in 10 years and small-growing plants where space is limited. (See page 58 for more about spacing.)

Low, spreading shrubs with horizontal branches, such as the Satsuki/Macrantha Hybrid azaleas, soften upright lines of houses and fences and keep your eye moving along the lines of the branches. Upright vase shapes, like those of the Knap Hill/Exbury Hybrid azaleas, stop your eye and break up monotonous horizontal lines. Plant several shrubs of the same shape in a group, and vary the groups to create visual excitement.

Mass plantings of azaleas of the same color produce a bold and dramatic effect.

The fact that many azaleas and rhododendrons achieve statuesque size at maturity should be considered when making plant selections for your garden.

White-flowering azaleas, planted en masse, offer a bright display in shady areas under densely branched trees.

Evergreen azalea hybrids enhance a formal entryway year-round; add visually refreshing color when they flower in spring.

'Sherwood Orchid' (Kurume Hybrid) has a spreading growth habit; bears violet-red flowers in midseason.

A WOODLAND GARDEN

Azaleas and rhododendrons grow naturally as shrubs in open forests on mountain slopes. There they enjoy the dappled light that diffuses through the branches of tall trees, and the moist but fast-draining, organically rich soil. It's quite feasible to create this natural setting, even on a small scale, in a typical suburban home landscape. A wooded setting of any size will display rhododendrons and azaleas like jewels against velvet.

To create a woodland garden, you need an area of your property shaded by high-branched trees planted fairly close together, similar to the manner they would grow in a woods. Trees must be deep-rooted, so they won't compete for water with the shrubs, and they should cast light filtered shade. (See the chart on page 14 for appropriate trees.) Evergreen shrubs and trees should be planted on the north side of the woodland, if the area is open to wind, to provide natural wind protection in areas with cold winters.

Depending upon the scale of your planting, choose large or small rhododendrons and azaleas. Plant them in scattered groups beneath the trees, adhering to the design principles outlined earlier on texture, color, and size.

The woodland garden is the perfect setting for native American azaleas and rhododendrons, though hybrids can be very effective too. You can interplant the azaleas and rhododendrons with smaller shrubs that bloom at different times of the year to create a longer color show. Wildflowers, spring-blooming bulbs, and ferns will be at home blanketing the open ground between the shrubs. (See pages 15 and 17 for companion shrubs and flowers that grow in acid soil in filtered shade.)

Such a natural woodland garden requires practically no attention once it is established. You should not even rake up fallen leaves since they add to the mulch that is so important in keeping soil rich, moist, and naturally acid.

A SHRUB BORDER

The borders of many yards are planted with shrubs to mark the boundaries and provide privacy, and simply because the borders of a property provide convenient planting sites for attractive plants. This bed of shrubs is called a shrub border and it can be as elaborate or as simple as the homeowner wishes. If the property border offers conditions suitable for azaleas and rhododendrons (see pages 19 to 22), this is an ideal place to display them.

Where there's room, the most effective borders are several shrubs deep and have curving shapes. Outlines with gentle curves where in-curves are balanced by out-curves are the most attractive. Arrange shrubs at several depths, creating a foreground, a midground, and a background. The plants in the front should be lower than those in the back, but it's best to avoid planting in rigid rows.

The shrub border can be planted only with azaleas and rhododendrons, in which case locate the taller, bolder rhododendrons as a dark green background for evergreen or deciduous azaleas, or plant them together at one end of the border. It's best to arrange several plants of one kind with harmonizing colors together, as described under the section on design basics. Shrub borders are most pleasing if they have a background such as a fence, wall, or backdrop of greenery from tall evergreens.

Choosing azaleas and rhododendrons that bloom at different times of the season will keep the border colorful. You may also wish to incorporate other flowering shrubs for variety and to keep the border in bloom throughout the summer. The chart of companion shrubs on page 15 lists plants that have the same requirements as azaleas and rhododendrons.

Borders of shrubs may also be planted along a house wall as a foundation planting or to accent a walkway or patio. In these cases, be extra careful to select plants that won't grow too tall or too wide, or they will soon outgrow the spaces intended for plants and crowd the spaces intended for people.

AN ORIENTAL GARDEN

An Oriental garden, despite its subtly formal elements, is really a simplified or stylized natural terrain. It could be thought of as a woodland garden pared down to its bare essentials. Few Westerners possess the knowledge or ability to construct an authentic Oriental garden with all its intricacies and symbolism. But the essential simplicity and serenity can be reproduced to please Western tastes.

Azaleas and rhododendrons are used sparingly as accents in Oriental gardens. You might group three low, fine-textured Kurumes that are sheared or pinched for compactness where they can mound over rocks. Satsuki/Macranthas and Kurumes are often pruned to accentuate their layered 'cloud' form. Locate a single deciduous azalea near a pool or fountain, or plant several of the same color in a mass. However, open space is essential and must strike a pleasing balance with planted areas.

COMPANION PLANTS

Plants that harmonize with azaleas and rhododendrons both culturally and aesthetically make good garden companions. When you consider possible companion trees, shrubs, ground covers, or perennials for azaleas and rhododendrons, follow these criteria: Companion plants should thrive in shade and acid soil and have water and fertilizer needs similar to those of azaleas and rhododendrons. A tree or large shrub should have a taproot rather than shallow, matting roots, which compete for water and nutrients. The companion plant's color and texture should not clash with the azaleas or rhododendrons you have in your garden.

On the following pages are lists of choice companion trees, shrubs, ground covers, and bulbs, 18 to 20 of each. The lists are by no means exhaustive.

The light airy branches of Mollis Hybrid azaleas create a graceful effect in Oriental gardens.

Spectacular color displays may be achieved by combining azaleas with flowers in complementary shades.

Japanese maple *(Acer palmatum),* a small graceful tree, is a visually pleasing backdrop for azaleas.

Dogwood trees *(Cornus sp.)* add a natural woodland feeling to azalea and rhododendron plantings.

COMPANION PLANTS: TREES

Name	Deciduous/ Evergreen	Height	*Recommended Zones:	Comments
Acer palmatum Japanese Maple	D	variable, to 20 ft	6-9 W 6-8 E	Beautiful graceful trees. Some have elegant deeply cut leaves, others have dark purple foliage. Beautiful red or yellow fall color. Trees may be too small to provide useful shade, but make exquisite companions. Protect from wind and drying sun in hot climates.
Amelanchier sp. Shadblow, Serviceberry	D	35 ft, or taller	4-8	Masses of fine-textured white flowers in early spring. Beautiful red fall color. Pinkish-gray trunk bark. Good shade from open, upright tree.
Cercis sp. Redbud	D	25-40 ft	5-9 W 4-8 E	Twigs, branches, and trunk bear clusters of small purplish-pink pealike flowers before heart-shaped leaves. White-flowering variety available.
Cornus sp. Dogwood	D	20-40 ft	5-9	Flowering dogwood, *C. florida,* blooms with azaleas. Clouds of white or pink blossoms. Prune high if used as shade, low for background. Japanese dogwood, *C. kousa,* produces white flowers a month later. Red fall color.
Eriobotrya japonica Loquat	E	20 ft	7-10	Large dark green leaves cast dense shade. Use as background. Golden fruits produced in early spring are edible and ornamental.
Gleditsia triacanthos inermis Thornless Honey Locust	D	60-90 ft	4-10 W 4-9 E	Airy tree with finely divided leaves. Casts light shade. Tolerates heat and drought. Leaves require little cleanup.
Ilex opaca American Holly	E	30-50 ft	6-9	Shiny, spiny foliage makes dense cover on pyramidal tree. Use as background and as windbreak. Berries form on female trees if pollinated.
Laburnum x watereri Golden-Chain Tree	D	25-30 ft	6-9 W 6-7 E	Long clusters of yellow wisterialike flowers in late spring. Prune to a single trunk to grow tall and cast light shade. Seeds are poisonous.
Larix sp. Larch	D	70-100 ft	5-8	Needles provide soft texture and light shade spring through fall; drop in autumn after changing to gold color. Several species available.
Magnolia x soulangiana Saucer Magnolia	D	20-25 ft	5-10	Large, fragrant white, pink, or purplish flowers in spring. Bold-textured leaves. Plant with azaleas and rhododendrons of compatible color.
Metasequoia glyptostroboides Dawn Redwood	D	75-85 ft	4-10	Small fine-textured needles drop in fall. Upright, open shape casts light shade. Fast-growing and graceful.
Oxydendrum arboreum Sourwood	D	15-25 ft, or taller	6-9	Clusters of tiny bell-like flowers in spring and ornamental seedpods in summer. Glossy green leaves turn scarlet in fall.
Pinus strobus White Pine	E	100-150 ft	2-8	Long bluish needles make fine-textured background. Tree casts light shade and makes good windbreak.
Pittosporum undulatum Victorian Box	E	15 ft, or taller	9-10	Handsome dark glossy green foliage. Makes good background and windbreak. Small inconspicuous flowers in spring are highly fragrant.
Prunus caroliniana Carolina Cherry Laurel	E	20-40 ft	7-10	Lush dark green background. May be sheared into hedge.
Pyrus calleryana 'Bradford' Bradford Pear	D	40-50 ft	5-9	Lovely lacy clusters of white flowers in early spring. Red foliage in fall. Good shade tree.
Quercus sp. Oak	D	60-80 ft	4-10	Red oak, *Q. rubra,* and scarlet oak, *Q. coccinea,* offer high open branching. Make good shade trees. Brilliant red fall color. Grow rapidly.
Rhus glabra Smooth Sumac	D	15 ft	3-8	Large, coarse-textured divided leaves in whorls. Striking red fall color. Makes useful background. Heat-tolerant.
Taxus baccata English Yew	E	40-60 ft	5-9 W 5-7 E	Dark green needles. Makes dense background as hedge or windbreak if pruned. Casts heavy shade as tree. Berry seeds are poisonous.
Tsuga sp. Hemlock	E	60-90 ft	5-9	Small, fine-textured, medium green needles. Tall gracefully drooping branches. Useful background and windbreak. Light shade.

See page 20 for locations of USDA Zones. Because climate patterns differ, zones are indicated for the West (W) and the East (E) where significant.

Viburnum *(Viburnum sp.)* is a good choice for interplanting, displaying azaleas and rhododendrons to beautiful advantage.

Dense-foliaged tobira *(Pittosporum tobira)* is widely used as a background shrub with azaleas and rhododendrons.

COMPANION PLANTS: SHRUBS

Name	Deciduous/ Evergreen	Height	*Recommended Zones:	Comments
Abelia x grandiflora Glossy Abelia	E/semi-D	6 ft	6-10	Dense growth. Small glossy leaves. Many small pink-tinged white flowers from summer to fall. Useful background. 'Edward Goucher' has purplish flowers.
Aucuba japonica Japanese Aucuba	E	6 to 10 ft	7-10	Bold glossy leaves, green or spotted with gold. Female plants may have bright red berries. Can be pruned to 3 ft. Needs shade.
Buxus sempervirens English Box	E	6-12 ft	5-10	Dense, glossy green leaves. May be sheared or pruned as desired. Makes fine-textured background.
Camellia sp. Camellia	E	5 to 10 ft	7-10	Useful for separating competing colors in borders and as background. Extends season by blooming in fall and winter. Pink, red, or white blossoms.
Gardenia jasminoides Gardenia	E	1 to 8 ft	8-10	Lustrous, dark green leaves. Fragrant white or ivory flowers in summer. Thrives in summer heat in some shade. 'Radicans', 1 foot tall, useful as foreground. Use taller 'Mystery' and 'Veitchii' in background.
Hamamelis x intermedia Witch Hazel	D	15-18 ft, or taller	6-9 W 6-8 E	Tall, open shrub. Very fragrant small feathery yellow or red flowers in late winter. Coarse foliage on zigzag branches; red or yellow fall color.
Hydrangea quercifolia Oakleaf Hydrangea	D	3 to 6 ft	6-9	Bold-textured leaves resemble oak leaves. Bright red fall color. Creamy-white flower clusters in midsummer extend floral season.
Ilex cornuta 'Burfordii' Burford Holly	E	10-14 ft	6-10	Dense, glossy, nearly spineless foliage. Red fall berries. Good background. *Ilex crenata*, Japanese holly, has small, shiny foliage. Resembles boxwood.
Kalmia latifolia Mountain Laurel	E	10 ft, or taller	5-8 W 5-9 E	Native American woodland shrub. Clusters of pink or white blossoms in June. Pointed leaves. Mix in border or woodland planting.
Leucothoe fontanesiana Drooping Leucothoe	E/semi-D	3 to 6 ft	5-8	Pointed bold-textured leaves. Bell-shaped white flowers in late spring. 'Scarletta', a dwarf hybrid, has bright red new growth; use in foreground.
Mahonia aquifolium Oregon Grape	E	2 to 6 ft	5-9 W 5-7 E	Bold-textured hollylike leaves. Clusters of yellow flowers in spring. Blue berries in fall and winter. New foliage red. Leaves reddish in winter.
Nandina domestica Heavenly Bamboo	E/semi-D	3 to 8 ft	6-10	Resembles bamboo, with delicate tall layers of divided leaves. Red fall color. Excellent background for low azaleas and dwarf rhododendrons.
Osmanthus heterophyllus Holly Olive	E	10 ft, or more	7-10	Resembles holly. Produces extremely fragrant, inconspicuous flowers during most of year. May be sheared into rounded shape for background.
Pieris japonica Japanese Andromeda	E	6 ft	5-9 W 5-8 E	Dense tapered leaves. Bell-shaped white flowers in early spring. Mountain andromeda, *P. floribunda*, is similar but more cold hardy.
Pittosporum tobira Tobira	E	6-15 ft, or more	8-10	Medium-sized, leathery green leaves may be variegated with white. Inconspicuous spring flowers are fragrant. 'Wheelers Dwarf' good in foreground.
Prunus tomentosa Nanking Cherry	D	9 ft	3-8	Good with deciduous azaleas. Single white flowers from pink buds in spring. Glossy green foliage. Plant has mounded shape.
Sarcococca hookerana humilis Sweet Box	E	5 to 6 ft	6-10 W 6-8 E	Small glossy leaves. Tiny, fragrant white flowers in early spring. Black berries in fall. Good with evergreen and deciduous azaleas.
Taxus cuspidata nana Dwarf Japanese Yew	E	2 to 3 ft, or taller	5-9 W 5-7 E	Dense dark green needles. Red berries in fall are poisonous. Can be sheared for formal effect.
Vaccinium ovatum Evergreen Huckleberry	E	5 to 10 ft	7	Resembles a loose, open boxwood. Foliage excellent background for deciduous azaleas. Can be pruned for formal look.
Viburnum sp. Viburnum	E	1 to 3 ft	8-10 W 8-9 E	Many species make excellent companion plants for woodlands or borders. White flowers in spring or early summer; red or black berries in fall; attractive summer foliage. Deciduous kinds usually have good fall color.

See page 20 for locations of USDA Zones. Because climate patterns differ, zones are indicated for the West (W) and the East (E) where significant.

Carpet bugle *(Ajuga reptans)* makes a colorful ground cover that is visually delightful with azaleas or rhododendrons.

Japanese spurge *(Pachysandra terminalis)* forms a dark green ground cover complementary to azaleas and rhododendrons.

COMPANION PLANTS: GROUND COVERS

Name	Deciduous/ Evergreen	Height	*Recommended Zones:	Comments
Ajuga reptans **Carpet Bugle**	D/E	4 to 10 inches	3-10	Dense carpets of quilted green, bronze, or purplish leaves. Spikes of blue, pink, or white flowers in spring. May be invasive.
Asarum sp. **Wild Ginger**	D/E	6 inches	3-9	Beautiful heart-shaped leaves carpet the ground. Roots can be ground into gingerlike spice. *A. canadense* is deciduous. *A. caudatum* and *A. europaeum* are evergreen and hardy to Zone 4.
Convallaria majalis **Lily-of-the-Valley**	D	8 inches	3-9	Lush carpet of upright, oval leaves. Delicate spikes of tiny, nodding, white flowers in spring. Fragrant. Poor ground cover in mild areas.
Duchesnea indica **Indian Mock Strawberry**	D/E	2 to 8 inches	6-10	Resembles strawberry with lobed scalloped-edged leaves. Yellow spring flowers and tasteless red berries.
Epimedium x rubrum **Epimedium**	E	8 to 12 inches	4-9	Wiry stems and delicate heart-shaped leaves. Clusters of cream or reddish spring flowers beneath the leaves.
Ferns **(many genera and species)**	D/E	6 inches to 6 ft or taller	variable	Many species of ferns are suitable for woodland gardens. They add a natural elegance and softening effect.
Gaultheria procumbens **Wintergreen**	E	3 to 6 inches	4-9	Native American ground cover. Mats of tiny glossy leaves. Inconspicuous flowers and showy red fall berries.
Heuchera sanguinea **Coralbells**	E	1 to 2 ft	4-10	Rounded toothed leaves hug the ground. Airy spikes of pink, red, or white flowers bloom in spring and summer.
Hosta sp. **Plantain Lily**	D	12 to 15 inches	4-9	Many species are grown for their clumps of beautiful foliage. Plants vary in size, have bright green, gray-green, blue-green, or variegated leaves. Spikes of lavender, purple, or white flowers in late summer or fall.
Iberis sempervirens **Edging Candytuft**	E	12 inches	4-10	Circles of white flowers create masses of white in early spring. Dark foliage beautiful year-round. 'Snowflake' has long blooming season.
Liriope muscari **Big Blue Lilyturf**	E	12 to 20 inches	7-10	Clumps of grassy foliage are green or green- and gold-striped. Spikes of purple, lavender, or white flowers in late summer or fall.
Myosotis sylvatica **Garden Forget-Me-Not**	D	10 to 20 inches	(annual) all zones	Tiny bright blue flowers with yellow eyes in spring and summer. An annual that reseeds and spreads.
Pachysandra terminalis **Japanese Spurge,** **Pachysandra**	E	6 to 12 inches	6-10 W 6-8 E	Whorls of dark green leaves. Makes thick dependable cover. Short spikes of white flowers in early summer. White berries.
Phlox stolonifera **Creeping Phlox**	E	6 to 12 inches	3-8	Perennial woodland wildflower. Forms thick cover of foliage. Loose clusters of delicate blue-violet flowers in spring.
Tiarella cordifolia **Allegheny Foamflower**	D	6 to 12 inches	4-7	Woodland wildflower. White flowers on 8- to 18-inch spikes in spring. Downy maplelike leaves close to the ground.
Vaccinium vitis-idaea **Cowberry**	E	8 to 12 inches	3-7	Low, creeping shrub with small shiny evergreen leaves. Tiny white spring flowers. Red fall berries. Good cover in light shade.
Vinca sp. **Periwinkle, Myrtle**	E	4 to 12 inches	5-10	Neat, glossy, oval leaves on creeping stems. Bright blue flowers in spring and early summer. 'Alba' is white-flowered form.
Viola sp. **Violet**	D/E	6 inches	5-10	Violets have heart-shaped leaves and spread by underground runners. Dainty blue, purple, or white flowers in spring.

*See page 20 for locations of USDA Zones. Because climate patterns differ, zones are indicated for the West (W) and the East (E) where significant.

Daylily (*Hemerocallis* hybrids) is a beautiful midsummer-blooming companion plant for azaleas and rhododendrons.

The clean, crisp appearance of daffodils (*Narcissus sp.*) contrasts superbly with plantings of azaleas or rhododendrons.

COMPANION PLANTS: BULBS

Name	Height	*Recommended Zones:	Planting Depth	Planting Time	Comments
Anemone blanda Windflower	3 to 8 inches	7-9	4 inches	fall	Many-petaled bright blue flowers with yellow stamens. Early spring. Downy, feathery leaves.
Chionodoxa luciliae Glory-of-the-Snow	3 to 6 inches	5-9	4 inches	September	Clusters of bright blue flowers with white eyes. Very early spring. Grasslike leaves. Plant under deciduous trees in full spring sun.
Clivia miniata Kaffir Lily	2 ft	10	tuber barely exposed	late spring	Bold clusters of brilliant orange flowers in spring. Thick glossy strap-shaped leaves. Good with white azaleas and ferns.
Colchicum autumnale Autumn Crocus	6 inches	4-10	4 inches	late summer	Fall-blooming chalice-shaped lavender, orchid, or white flowers. Foliage appears in spring and dies in summer.
Crocus vernus Dutch Crocus	3 to 5 inches	3-10	4 inches	September	Early-spring purple, lavender, white, or yellow cuplike blossoms. Many varieties available. Multiplies readily.
Cyclamen hederifolium, Baby Cyclamen	4 inches	6-10 W 6-8 E	2 inches	July	Small, unusual summer flowers with twisted, backswept petals. Red or white. Leathery, mottled leaves close to the ground.
Eranthis hyemalis Winter Aconite	8 inches	5-8	2 inches	late summer	Carpets of yellow buttercuplike flowers in very early spring. Whorls of leaves die to ground in summer. Can invade lawn. Poisonous if eaten.
Erythronium sp. Dog-Tooth Violet	6 inches	3-8	2 to 4 inches	fall	Woodland wildflower with mottled leaves. Small lilylike blossoms in yellow, white, or rosy-purple. Several species available.
Galanthus sp. Snowdrop	12 inches	4-9	4 inches	late summer or early fall	White drooping flowers with flared petals marked with green. Early spring. Grassy foliage. *G. nivalis* is daintier and earlier than *G. elwesii.*
Hemerocallis hybrids Daylily	1 to 5 ft	3-10	cover roots	early spring, fall	Clumps of strap-shaped foliage. Large orange, yellow, pink, bronze, or reddish flowers in midsummer. Naturalize on woodland edge.
Iris cristata Crested Iris	3 to 4 inches	4-8	on surface	fall	A dwarf iris native to Appalachian Mts. Blue, yellow, or white flowers with yellow crests. Early spring. Use in border or woodland.
Leucojum sp. Snowflake	12 inches	5-9	3 inches	September	White bell-like flowers, grassy foliage. *L. vernum* blooms in spring; *L. aestivum* in summer; *L. autumnale* in fall.
Lilium canadense Canada Lily	3 to 5 ft	4-9	5 inches	fall	Native woodland lily. Golden blossoms in July. Use in border or naturalistic setting.
Lycoris squamigera Magic Lily	2 ft	6-10 W 6-9 E	5 inches	August	Foliage emerges in spring, dies in summer. Stalks of fragrant rose-lilac flowers seem to sprout from bare earth in late summer.
Muscari sp. Grape Hyacinth	6 to 12 inches	5-10	2 inches	late summer or early fall	Dense spikes of rounded purplish-blue flowers in early spring. Grassy foliage. Plant along borders or on edge of woodland.
Narcissus sp. Narcissus, Daffodil	18 inches	5-10	6 inches	fall	White, yellow, or golden flowers with contrasting trumpets or cups. Blooms in spring. Mix in borders or naturalize in woodland.
Scilla sp. Squill	6 inches	3-10	4 inches	fall	Tall stalks of blue flowers in summer. Pink, white, and lavender kinds available. *S. hispanica,* bell-shaped; *S. siberica,* fringed.
Trillium sp. Trillium	18 inches	4-7	10 inches	early fall	Native wildflowers with 3-petalled white or purple blossoms above whorl of 3 leaves. Naturalize in woodland. Spring blooming.
Tulipa turkestanica Turkscap Tulip	12 inches	5-10	6 inches	fall	Loose clusters of yellow starlike flowers marked with white. Early spring. Good for foreground of border or edge of woodland.
Zephyranthes sp. Rain Lily	10 inches	7-10	1 to 2 inches	fall	Beautiful lilylike white or pale purplish flowers in late summer or early fall after a rain. Needs some sun.

*See page 20 for locations of USDA Zones. Because climate patterns differ, zones are indicated for the West (W) and the East (E) where significant.

LIMITATIONS

It's not so difficult to extend the natural limits of many azaleas and rhododendrons once you understand just how climate factors are limiting their growth in your garden. You can manipulate the environment a little bit to your advantage by using some tricks learned by expert gardeners.

Temperature: Minimum winter temperature has long been the traditional basis for gauging adaptability of azaleas and rhododendrons. You can get a pretty fair assessment of whether or not a particular plant will grow in your garden if you know your hardiness zone and the cold limit of the plant. Temperatures however vary within a region and microclimates occur wherever elevation, bodies of water, sun exposure, and heat-absorbing materials such as rock outcroppings or buildings are substantial enough to influence temperature. For instance, cities are always warmer than their surrounding suburbs because the roads and buildings heat up from the sun during the day and slowly radiate the heat back all night. Areas bordering large lakes are warmer in fall and colder in spring than surrounding areas.

Around your home and property, there are small, localized temperature and moisture changes, called microclimates, that can spell the difference between death and survival for many azaleas and rhododendrons. Plants that are borderline hardy for your area may perish if planted in a cold microclimate, but thrive if planted in a warm one.

Warm microclimates: The south-facing side of your home, if unshaded by trees, is a warm microclimate. Such a location could be a good spot for borderline plants because it is much warmer in winter than the rest of the property; however, direct sun would be too hot and drying year-round for azaleas and rhododendrons. The north or east side of a house, better exposures for azalea and rhododendron growth, can be warmed up with a large paved surface such as a patio or driveway. This is a better planting spot for borderline plants.

Other suitable warm spots are east- or west-facing slopes, and the edges of large bodies of water that don't freeze in winter. South-facing slopes, though warm, are usually too hot and dry for successful growth.

Cold microclimates: Planting spots to avoid are those that are colder than other areas on your property. Low-lying spots act as frost-pockets because cold air sinks, draining from high ground and collecting at the bottom of a slope or in a depression. These pockets are the first places frost occurs in fall and the last places frost occurs in spring. Plants growing in frost pockets may be expecting warmer weather at the time of these early and late frosts and will be injured.

Temperature fluctuations: The gradually colder and shorter days of autumn signal plants to prepare for winter's cold. Chemical changes begin within the plant that enable the tissues to endure freezing temperatures. A reverse process happens in spring. Any sharp temperature changes in late winter or early spring can interfere with the plant's dormancy and have disastrous effects on certain plants. A warm spell late in winter can break a plant's dormancy, causing its buds to swell. When cold returns, the tissues are unprepared and the flower buds may be injured. This is particularly true of early-flowering varieties, which are quick to break dormancy in spring.

Ironically, a plant well adapted to the consistent winter cold of Maine may be damaged in Alabama by a cold snap in early spring. In the mild climate, the plant is only weakly dormant and any warm weather gets it growing in spring, only to be startled by an onset of cold weather. Plants growing in warm microclimates may also break dormancy early in spring.

In regions where dormancy is likely to be interrupted by warm spells, consider planting late-blooming varieties and species. They are less likely to break dormancy early. Northern exposures out of warming spring sun also prolong dormancy and in such a cold microclimate plants are slower to react to early mild spells.

Early frosts in fall, before plants are fully dormant, can also be injurious. To help shrubs resist early fall frost, plants should be hardened off. Water less at the end of the summer and don't apply fertilizer containing nitrogen after midsummer because both water and fertilizer stimulate growth—in fall plants should be slowing down and beginning dormancy.

MORE THAN COLD

It's not always the cold by itself that does a plant in. Each plant of course does have its cold-tolerance limit, but that limit is affected by many other climate factors such as sun, water, wind, and as previously mentioned, temperature fluctuations. These factors can influence the degree of a plant's dormancy and hence its ability to withstand cold.

Winter sun and wind: When the soil is frozen, no water is available for plants to take up through their roots. Hot sun and wind cause plants to lose water, to some extent from their stems, but to a much larger extent through their foliage. Evergreens are very susceptible to drying out in winter because they lose water readily through their leaves and may not be able to replenish it. During prolonged cold, sunny spells, azaleas and rhododendrons can become desiccated. Wind is such a severe problem that in many cold areas a plant growing near a windy corner of a house may be dried out and killed, while a similar plant only a few feet away, but out of the wind, is unharmed.

One way rhododendrons cope with cold weather is by curling their leaves. Leaf curling reduces the surface exposed to drying sun and wind and thus slows water loss. A rhododendron is a good weather

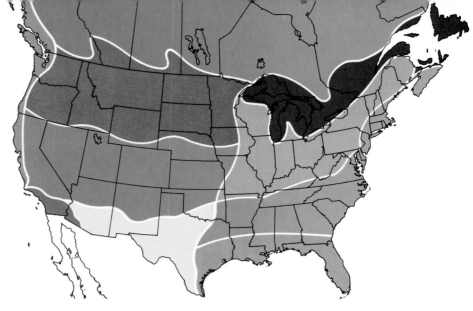

barometer, since you can simply glance out your window and get a good idea of the temperature by how much the leaves are curled—the colder the weather, the more the leaves droop and curl.

Plants that are well-watered when soil freezes are better able to withstand winter sun and wind. If the season is dry, it's a good idea to water shrubs heavily in fall after the first frost—earlier watering may slow the onset of dormancy. If snow is unusually scant, water plants in exposed sites during thaws.

Planting azaleas and rhododendrons where they are protected from strong winds by a windbreak of evergreen trees or a fence or wall will also help them survive the winter. Selecting a planting location out of direct winter sun can be tricky. The angle of the sun changes in winter and deciduous trees drop their leaves. Provide sufficient winter shade when planting azaleas and rhododendrons.

HOT CLIMATES

It's generally true that most evergreen azaleas fare better in areas where summer heat is high than do rhododendrons and deciduous azaleas. In the South, it is not always the heat, but often a soil fungus that causes the plants to suffer. Fungus organisms are most likely to attack roots in warm climates where soil is poorly drained. In such climates, avoid unnecessary watering, and be sure soil is fast-draining. By growing these shrubs in raised beds of suitable soil, you can often avoid fungus problems in hot, humid areas. (See pages 55 and 62.) Some southern gardeners recommend a fungicidal soil drench at planting time.

In the Southwest, climates often are too hot and dry for azaleas and rhododendrons. Many gardeners in these areas have success with azaleas by watering them frequently, hosing and misting the foliage to raise the humidity and cool the plants during the heat of the day, and by planting in shaded locations protected from drying wind.

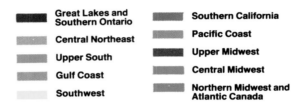
UNSUITABLE SOIL

Alkaline and clay soils are perhaps just as limiting in their own way as cold temperatures. Azaleas and rhododendrons need acid, fast-draining soil. Alkaline soil binds iron and manganese in forms that azaleas and rhododendrons cannot use, so they suffer from nutrient deficiency. These plants have delicate, shallow roots that cannot penetrate heavy soil and their growth is severely curtailed. Where soil drains poorly, azalea and rhododendron roots suffer from lack of oxygen.

If you live in an area where soil is unsuitable, such as the alkaline areas of the Southwest or the clay soil areas of Southern California, you can still grow azaleas and rhododendrons—albeit with some extra effort. Planting in raised beds or planters containing a suitable soil is the answer. See page 55 for more information on soil and raised beds.

REGIONAL CHOICES

Different regions of the country are better suited to azaleas and rhododendrons than others, and each region has its own choice of top-rated plants. The map above will make it easy to select the best azaleas and rhododendrons for your yard and garden. The map divides the United States and Canada into 10 growing regions. The regions differ in amount of rainfall, soil conditions, humidity, length of growing season, and other climate factors of significance to azalea and rhododendron culture. The charts on the following pages list regions where top-rated azaleas and rhododendrons are adapted. You can use the Hardiness Zone Map and the Regional Map to determine which region and which hardiness zone you live in. Then use the lists to select the best plants for your garden.

In some cases you'll notice that the minimum temperature given in the plant lists is colder than the low temperature for the listed zones. All temperatures are of course approximate (the USDA zone temperatures represent an average over the last 100 years) and a plant's hardiness will vary slightly from year to year depending upon other climate factors. Use these temperatures and zones as a guideline, but not as hard-and-fast laws. Experimentation may bring surprising and pleasing results.

Azaleas: Regional Recommendations

	Minimum Temperature (degrees F)	Recommended Zones	Great Lakes and Southern Ontario	Central Northeast	Upper South	Gulf Coast	Southwest	Southern California	Pacific Coast	Upper Midwest	Central Midwest	Northern Midwest and Atlantic Canada
HYBRIDS												
Belgian Indica Hybrids (E)	20°	8-10		■	■	■		■	■			
Gable Hybrids (E)	0°	6-8	■	■	■				■			
Ghent Hybrids (D)	−25°	4-8	■	■	■				■			
Girard Hybrids (E)	−5°	6-9	■	■	■				■	■		
Glenn Dale Hybrids (E)	5°	7-9		■	■			■	■	■		
Gold Cup, Brooks, Nuccio Hybrids (E)	20°	9-10					■*	■				
Kaempferi Hybrids (E)	−10°	5-9	■		■					■		
Knap Hill/Exbury Hybrids (D)	−20°	5-8		■	■				■			
Kurume Hybrids (E)	5°	7-10		■	■			■	■			
Mollis Hybrids (D)	−20°	5-8	■		■				■			
Northern Lights Hybrids (D)	−45°	3-4	■	■						■	■	■
Occidentale Hybrids (D)	−25°	6-8		■	■				■			
Pericat Hybrids (E)	5°	7-10			■			■	■			
Rutherfordiana Hybrids (E)	20°	8-10						■	■			
Satsuki/Macrantha Hybrids (E)	5°	7-10			■			■	■			
Southern Indica Hybrids (E)	20°	8-10				■	■*	■				
SPECIES												
R. arborescens	−20°	5-9	■	■	■	■			■			
R. atlanticum	−10°	6-9		■	■	■			■			
R. austrinum	−10°	6-10		■	■				■			
R. bakeri	−20°	5-8	■	■	■				■			
R. calendulaceum	−20°	5-8	■	■	■				■			
R. canadense	−40°	3-7	■	■	■				■	■		■
R. japonicum	−25°	5-8	■	■	■	■			■			
R. luteum	−25°	6-8	■	■	■				■			
R. molle	−20°	6-8		■	■				■			
R. occidentale	−5°	7-9						■	■			
R. periclymenoides	−30°	4-9	■	■	■				■	■	■	■
R. prinophyllum	−30°	4-8	■	■	■				■	■		■
R. prunifolium	−10°	7-9			■				■			
R. schlippenbachii	−25°	5-9	■	■	■				■		■	
R. serrulatum	0°	7-10			■	■						
R. vaseyi	−30°	5-9	■	■	■	■			■	■		■
R. viscosum	−30°	4-9	■	■	■	■			■			
R. yedoense var. poukhanense	−5°	6-8	■	■	■							

*Plant in raised beds or containers filled with fast-draining, acid soil mix (page 55).

'Scintillation' rhododendron

'Anah Kruschke' rhododendron

Rhododendrons: Regional Recommendations

	Minimum Temperature (degrees F)	Recommended Zones	Great Lakes and Southern Ontario	Central Northeast	Upper South	Gulf Coast	Southwest	Southern California	Pacific Coast	Upper Midwest	Central Midwest	Northern Midwest and Atlantic Canada
HYBRIDS												
'Arthur Bedford'	− 5°	7-8		■	■				■			
'America'	−20°	5-8	■	■	■				■	■	■	
'Anah Kruschke'	−10°	6-8		■	■			■	■			
'Anna Rose Whitney'	− 5°	7-8	■	■	■	■			■			
'Antoon van Welie'	− 5°	7-8	■		■			■	■			
'Blue Ensign'	−10°	6-8						■				
'Blue Jay'	− 5°	7-8			■				■			
'Blue Peter'	−10°	6-8		■	■							
'Boule de Neige'	−25°	5-8	■	■	■			■	■	■	■	■
'Bow Bells'	0°	7-8						■	■			
'Bric-a-Brac'	5°	8-9			■				■			
'Caractacus'	−25°	5-8	■	■	■				■	■	■	■
'Carmen'	− 5°	7-8							■			
'Caroline'	−15°	6-8		■	■				■			
'Catawbiense Album'	−25°	5-8	■	■	■			■	■		■	■
'Chionoides'	−20°	5-8	■	■	■			■	■	■		■
'Cunningham's White'	−10°	6-8	■	■	■				■			
'Daphnoides'	−10°	6-8		■	■				■			
'Dr. V.H. Rutgers'	−20°	5-8		■	■				■			
'Dora Amateis'	−15°	6-9	■	■	■				■			
'English Roseum'	−20°	5-8	■	■	■				■	■	■	■
'Fastuosum Flore Pleno'	−10°	6-8		■	■				■			
'Fragrantissimum'	20°	9-10					■*	■	■			
'General Eisenhower'	0°	7-8		■					■			
'Gomer Waterer'	−15°	6-8	■	■	■			■	■	■	■	■
'Graf Zeppelin'	0°	7-8		■	■				■			
'Herbert Parsons'	−25°	5-8	■	■	■				■	■	■	■

*Plant in raised beds or containers filled with fast-draining, acid soil mix (page 55)

	Minimum Temperature (degrees F)	Recommended Zones	Great Lakes and Southern Ontario	Central Northeast	Upper South	Gulf Coast	Southwest	Southern California	Pacific Coast	Upper Midwest	Central Midwest	Northern Midwest and Atlantic Canada
'Humming Bird'	0°	7-9							■			
'Ignatius Sargent'	−20°	5-8	■	■	■				■	■	■	■
'Janet Blair'	−15°	6-8		■	■				■			
'Kluis Sensation'	0°	7-8		■	■				■			
'Lee's Dark Purple'	−20°	5-8	■	■	■	■			■		■	■
'Moonstone'	0°	7-9		■	■				■			
'Mother of Pearl'	0°	7-9										
'Mrs. Charles E. Pearson'	−5°	7-8		■	■				■			
'Mrs. Furnival'	−10°	6-8	■	■	■				■			
'Nova Zembla'	−25°	5-8	■	■	■				■		■	■
'Parson's Gloriosum'	−25°	5-8	■	■	■				■		■	
'Pink Pearl'	−5°	7-8			■	■		■	■			
'P.J.M.'	−25°	5-8	■	■	■				■		■	■
'Purple Gem'	−15°	6-8	■		■				■			
'Purple Splendor'	−10°	6-8			■	■		■	■			
'Ramapo'	−20°	5-8	■	■	■				■		■	
'Roseum Elegans'	−25°	5-8	■	■	■	■		■	■		■	
'Sappho'	−5°	7-8		■	■			■	■			
'Scarlet Wonder'	−10°	6-8							■			
'Scintillation'	−10°	6-8	■	■	■				■			
'The Hon. Jean Marie de Montague'	0°	7-8		■	■	■		■	■			
'Trilby'	−10°	6-8		■	■				■			
'Unique'	0°	7-8			■				■			
'Vulcan'	−5°	7-8	■	■	■				■			
'Windbeam'	−25°	5-8	■	■	■				■			
'Yaku King'	−10°	6-8	■	■	■				■			
'Yaku Prince'	−10°	6-8	■	■	■				■			
'Yaku Princess'	−10°	6-8	■	■	■				■			
'Yaku Queen'	−10°	6-8	■	■	■				■			
SPECIES												
R. carolinianum	−25°	5-8	■	■	■				■		■	
R. catawbiense	−25°	4-8	■	■	■				■			
R. chryseum	−15°	6-7							■			
R. fastigiatum	−15°	6-8							■			
R. impeditum	−15°	6-8	■		■				■		■	
R. intricatum	−15°	6-8										
R. keiskei	−5°	7-8		■	■				■		■	
R. keleticum	−10°	6-8								■	■	
R. maximum	−25°	5-8	■	■	■				■	■	■	■
R. moupinense	−5°	7-9						■	■			
R. mucronulatum	−15°	5-8	■	■	■						■	
R. pemakoense	0°	7-8							■			
R. yakusimanum	−15°	6-8	■	■					■	■		

Top-Rated Azaleas

Azaleas are extremely popular flowering shrubs, second in popularity only to roses. They are ideal plants for home landscapes, providing glorious color in spring and handsome leaves or branches the rest of the year. Use them as serviceable foundation plants, in decorative shrub borders, and in naturalistic woodland gardens. Wherever you plant azaleas, they will be sure to reward you for many years with their abundant blossoms.

There are 70 distinct species of azaleas within the large and complex genus *Rhododendron*. And the named hybrids, which fall into many distinct hybrid groups, number several thousand. This large number of azaleas might surprise many people who are familiar only with the azaleas that grow in their area.

Depending upon where you live, only a limited number may be adapted to your climate. For instance, in Southern California, gardeners are largely restricted to Belgian Indica and Southern Indica varieties, which tolerate the heat and dryness. In the Great Lakes area, gardeners know the cold hardy deciduous Ghent Hybrids best. On the other hand, in prime azalea territory, the choice is enormous. The following pages contain descriptions of evergreen azalea hybrid groups and deciduous azalea hybrid groups. The main characteristics of each hybrid group are discussed. The chart on page 23 rates azaleas according to the regions where they are adapted.

At left: Mollis Hybrid azaleas bear clusters of flowers that may be colored yellow, salmon, orange, pink, or red.

Plum-leaved azalea *(R. prunifolium)*

'Daviesii' (Ghent Hybrid)

'Pink Pearl' (Kurume Hybrid)

'Hinodegiri' (Kurume Hybrid)

EVERGREEN AZALEA HYBRID GROUPS

Many groups of hybrid azaleas are available, offering home gardeners a vast choice of plants. Each hybrid group was bred with specific goals in mind, such as larger flowers, more cold hardiness, or particular plant forms or flower colors.

Depending upon the group and the climate, evergreen azaleas retain differing numbers of leaves during the winter. Hybrids for southern areas have larger leaves and retain a full complement of leaves throughout the winter. In colder areas, evergreen kinds have smaller leaves and a finer texture. In fall, older inner leaves change color and drop, leaving varying amounts of foliage to cloak the branches in winter. The overwintering foliage often takes on beautiful reddish or purplish hues, depending upon the variety.

The hybrid groups described below are arranged in order of least to most cold hardy.

Belgian Indica Hybrids

These tender evergreen azaleas (hardy only to 20°F) were bred in Belgium, as well as in France, Germany, and England, beginning in the 1830's. The first parents were Japanese and Chinese imports brought to Europe by trading companies. They were bred for greenhouse forcing, though they easily adapted to growing outdoors in mild climates. The showiness of their profuse double, semidouble, or frilled flowers makes them modern-day favorites in southern gardens and for florist gift plants.

Southern Indica Hybrids

Southern Indicas were America's first evergreen azaleas and were introduced by the P. J. Berkman's Company of Augusta, Georgia.

AZALEA FLOWER FORMS

Azalea and rhododendron flowers, in their simplest forms, consist of five petals fused at their base into a short tube with five lobes. Azaleas flowers can have one of six shapes.

Single flowers are simple funnel-shaped forms created by five fused petals. Semidouble and double flowers have extra petals created by the stamens becoming petallike. In double flowers, all or nearly all of the stamens look like petals. Hose-in-hose flowers form when the sepals, "leaves" at the base of the petals, become petallike, forming a second funnel around the funnel of petals. Semidouble and double hose-in-hose flowers have both two funnels of petals and petallike stamens in their centers. Frilled flowers are characterized by petal edges that are ruffled or wavy.

Often a variety, 'Hinodegiri' for instance, that usually has single flowers will develop at different times or at one time single, semidouble, and double flowers. Factors such as climate and cultural conditions, along with genetic proclivity, determine when and to what degree the transformation occurs. Flower "doubling" is more common as growing conditions approach optimum.

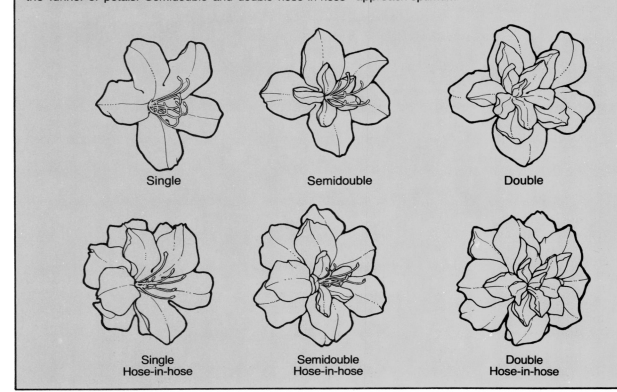

Single

Semidouble

Double

Single
Hose-in-hose

Semidouble
Hose-in-hose

Double
Hose-in-hose

(The company was later renamed Fruitland Nursery.) Specimens planted in the mid-1800's at Magnolia Gardens and other famous plantation gardens are still the stars of the spring show.

Similar in appearance to Belgian Indicas, these plants grow taller and faster, and tolerate more sun. Hardy to temperatures of 20°F.

Brooks Hybrids: These are tender hybrids (hardy to 20°F) of Belgian Indicas, Kurumes, and species such as *R. mucronulatum* and *R. indicum*. Lenard L. Brooks of Modesto, California, spent a quarter-century breeding these plants. Mr. Brooks' primary interest was developing azaleas adaptable to the hot summers and mild winters of California's Central Valley. Other aims were compact habit and good foliage and flower form.

About 30 of Mr. Brooks' varieties have reached the marketplace. A few, such as top-rated 'Redwing', have become very popular, but some confusion surrounds them. Some nursery catalogs list 'Redwing' simply as "hybrid" and others include it among Pericat, Kurume, or Rutherfordiana Hybrids. The Brooks Hybrids, like the Gold Cup and Nuccio Hybrids, are most often mistakenly listed as belonging to other more familiar groups.

Nuccio Hybrids: Nurseryman Julius Nuccio of Altadena, California has used the florist's azalea to breed reliable garden plants for his climate. Sun tolerance, vigor, sturdy root systems, and fragrance are prime virtues he sought. 'Nuccio's Pink Champagne', released in the mid-1960's, was one of the first. Lavender 'Happy Days' is popular in Southern California today. No Nuccio Hybrids (hardy to 20°F) are top-rated, only because they are not widely available. If you live in Southern California, visit Nuccio's Nursery in Altadena to see or obtain them.

Gold Cup Hybrids: Like the Brooks and Nuccio Hybrids, these azaleas are hybrids of the tender (20°F) Belgian Indica, Southern Indica, and Rutherfordiana Hybrids. Developed by Lynn Mossholder of Southern California, they are late-blooming, large-flowered, compact azaleas. None are top-rated due to limited availability, even in Southern California, but 'Sun Valley', with shiny white flowers with a green throat, is most often available.

Rutherfordiana Hybrids

These plants were American-bred for greenhouse forcing by Bobbink and Atkins Nursery of East Rutherford, N.J. They are 4-foot-tall, vigorous plants with flowers larger than the Belgian Indicas. Cold hardy to 20°F, they adapt well to outdoor culture in suitable climates. Blossoms are single, double, or semidouble.

Kurume Hybrids

These are Japanese hybrids whose breeding began in the early 1800's in the Japanese city of Kurume. Their parents are species native to the windswept peaks of Mt. Kirishima.

Cold hardy to 5°F, Kurume azaleas offer neat, tidy leaves and masses of small flowers. Flowers are single or hose-in-hose. Plants can grow quite large and tall, and branches are often layered in tiers.

Kurumes were first seen in the Western world in 1915 at the Panama Pacific Exposition in San Francisco. They received a gold medal, but otherwise little public attention, though Toichi Domoto of Domoto Brothers Nursery in Hayward, California obtained exclusive importation rights. Several of the hybrids he imported, such as 'Christmas Cheer', 'Coral Bells', and 'Snow', remain top-rated today.

In 1918, "Chinese" Wilson traced Kurumes to their source in Japan, where he selected 50 hybrids that he sent back to the Arnold Arboretum in Boston. These became known as the "Wilson Fifty." Later the United States Department of Agriculture imported 50 more. After Kurume azaleas were exhibited in 1920 at the Massachusetts Horticultural Society, they became great North American garden favorites.

Pericat Hybrids

This group was created by florist Alphonse Pericat of Collingdale, Pennsylvania for greenhouse forcing. They are however surprisingly cold hardy plants, tolerating 5°F, and so are good garden shrubs. Unfortunately, only a few varieties of these clear-colored azaleas are available, but one, 'Sweetheart Supreme', is top-rated.

Satsuki/Macrantha Hybrids

Created by Japanese hybridizers as early as the seventeenth century, this group is also known, confusingly, as Indica Hybrids (not Belgian or Southern Indicas) and Macrantha Hybrids. "Satsuki" translates from Japanese as "fifth month" indicating that these plant are late blooming. Large, often frilly flowers and dwarf, sometimes pendant form have made them favorite bonsai subjects in Japan. Their attractiveness and hardiness to 5°F have made them popular in North America.

Glenn Dale Hybrids

Hybridized at the USDA Plant Introduction Station at Glenn Dale, Maryland, by Dr. B.Y. Morrison, former director of the National Arboretum, these plants were bred for survival in the Mid-Atlantic States. Using a number of commercially available varieties and species and hybrids imported from Japan, he began breeding in 1929. The first varieties were introduced around 1940.

They are the largest group of evergreen azaleas and over 400 varieties of Glenn Dales are available today. They include plants of varying size, habit, and flower characteristics, but all are hardy to approximately 5°F. Some varieties are partially deciduous through the coldest winters.

Gable Hybrids

This hardy group was developed by Joseph B. Gable of Stewartstown, Pennsylvania. He introduced the first of them in 1927. Among the hardy species he used in hybridizing were the Korean azalea, *R. poukhanense*, and Kaempfer azalea, *R. kaempferi*. But parentage of the individual members of the group, like that of the Satsuki/Macrantha Hybrids, varies so much that their only common characteristic is hardiness—to between −5° and 0°F. (A few are hardy to −10°F.)

Girard Hybrids

These hybrids, introduced in recent decades by Peter E. Girard of Girard Bros. Nursery in Geneva, Ohio, are offspring of Gables crossed with *R. mucronatum*, *R. poukhanense*, and others. Girard's first objective was hardiness—his avowed goal was to produce azaleas hardy enough for the coldest areas of Wisconsin. However this group is not much hardier than the Gables—about −5F.

Kaempferi Hybrids

These are unusually hardy (to −10°F) evergreen hybrids. Known as the Malvatica Hybrids in Holland and England, they are primarily offspring of *R. kaempferi*, a 10-foot Japanese azalea, and the Malvatica Hybrids, azaleas of unknown parentage. They grow vigorously to 8 feet and bloom freely. Kaempferi Hybrids were created in the second decade of the twentieth century by P.M. Koster and C.B. Van Nes and Sons of Boskoop, Holland.

DECIDUOUS AZALEA HYBRID GROUPS

The deciduous azaleas are known for their clusters of often fiery-colored blossoms that decorate bare branches in early spring. They are tall, open plants and usually offer excellent foliage colors in fall before leaves drop. Some varieties have fragrant flowers.

Knap Hill/Exbury Hybrids

Around 1870 Anthony Waterer, eminent English horticulturist, crossed *R. molle* from China with the flame azalea from America. To this blend he eventually added Ghent Hybrids and several American species, including the western azalea, *R. occidentale*. The resulting Knap Hill Hybrids, named for his nursery, were brilliant. Their durable, fragrant flowers, larger than Ghent Hybrid flowers, were in soft to flaming-hot tones, many with contrasting darker crests.

For a long time Knap Hill Hybrids received little notice, but in the 1920's they began to attract the attention of several talented horticulturists: the Slocock family of Goldsworth Old Nursery, near Waterer's nursery; Edgar Stead of the Ilam Estate near Christchurch, New Zealand; and Lionel de Rothschild of Exbury, in Surrey, England. These horticulturists refined the already brilliant results of Waterer's work, and created the Slocock, Ilam, Knap Hill, and Exbury strains or subgroups of the Knap Hill Hybrids. (Adding to the confusion, the original Knap Hill Hybrids and the three groups developed from them are all often collectively called Knap Hill Hybrids!)

Many azalea growers consider Exburys the ultimate hybrid. And certainly their creation by de Rothschild represents one of the titanic—and successful—undertakings in horticultural history. The international banker/horticulturist selected and crossed Knap Hill Hybrids for years, on a scale that defies imagination, and with remarkable single-mindedness. Every year he brought hundreds of thousands of Knap Hill seedlings into bloom—then kept two of each color and burned the rest. His annual late-spring fires became famous around the Surrey countryside. Each spared plant was added to his superior breeding stock. Finally he had 104 named varieties too good for burning. Resplendent colors and combinations of colors, elegant markings, broad, 5-inch flowers in massive clusters, and brilliant fall foliage on the 3- to 5-foot shrubs, hardy to −20°F, have rewarded their creator's efforts.

Mollis Hybrids

These azaleas, hardy to −20°F, were created in the 1870's in Belgium and Holland from *R. molle* from China, *R. japonicum* from Japan, and perhaps other species and hybrids, including North American *R. viscosum*, swamp azalea. Members of the Koster family, prominent Dutch horticulturists, produced some of the most outstanding varieties in the 1890's. The 4- to 6-foot shrubs are generally heat-tolerant and produce clusters of single yellow, salmon, orange, pink, or red flowers.

Occidentale Hybrids

R. occidentale, the Western azalea, was discovered in 1827. It is found along mountain streams from southern Oregon to southern California at altitudes usually in excess of 5,000 feet. Forty years later in England it was crossed with *R. molle* and various Mollis Hybrids by Anthony Waterer. The group of plants that resulted, known as the Albicans Hybrids, have mostly disappeared, but similar crosses in Holland and England in the early 1900's created the group presently known as the Occidentale Hybrids. Hardy to −25°F, these hybrids frequently are listed as either Ghent or even Knap Hill/Exbury Hybrids.

Ghent Hybrids

Among the most cold hardy of the azaleas, these hybrids from Ghent, Belgium, are tolerant of −25°F. They were developed in the 1820's from several American species: the gold-flowered flame azalea, *R. calendulaceum*, and the pink-flowered pinxterbloom azalea, *R. periclymenoides*. Later, in England, the very fragrant yellow-flowered pontic azalea, *R. luteum*, from the Caucasus, and the pink-flowered swamp azalea, *R. viscosum*, from America, were added to the breeding stock. These hybrids, along with crosses from other American species, form the Ghent azaleas. Plants grow to 6 feet. Double-flowered forms have been developed.

Northern Lights Hybrids

This is a relatively new group of azaleas bred for hardiness to extreme cold. Developed at the University of Minnesota Landscape Arboretum at Chaska, Minnesota, they are the only winter-hardy azaleas that reliably bloom in the upper Midwest. Flower buds withstand temperatures as low as −45°F (Zone 3).

Mature height and width of plants is 6 to 7 feet. They produce 1-1/2-inch clustered flowers in late May or early June. Each cluster includes up to one dozen flowers and is 3 to 4 inches wide. Leaves are 1 inch wide, 3 to 4 inches long, and deciduous.

Presently, Northern Lights Hybrids are available in very limited quantities, so are not top-rated. Available plants are all seedlings.

This means each plant will show minor differences in form, size, and flower color. Named varieties 'Pink Lights', 'Rosy Lights', and 'White Lights' (slightly less hardy, to −35°F) will be available soon.

SELECTION GUIDE TO THE TOP-RATED AZALEAS

In the following charts are descriptions of the top-rated azaleas. These are varieties that have been selected both for their beauty and their durability. They are the best plants for home gardeners because they are easy to care for and readily available. You should find the ones suitable for your area at your local garden center or nursery.

The charts provide descriptions of the flowers and the plant size and shape, and give the all-important season of bloom. For a long display, it's a good idea to choose a selection of azaleas that bloom several weeks

apart. You may also want to select late-blooming azaleas, if you live in a cold area, to prevent injury from late spring frosts, or if you want to grow azaleas beyond their limit of cold hardiness. (See page 31.)

Unlike the rhododendron charts, the azalea charts have no ratings of flower and plant quality by the American Rhododendron Society. Very few azaleas are rated at this time. However, the society is beginning to rate azaleas in the same way they do rhododendrons, and in a few years many of the azaleas at your nursery will be rated.

The charts are organized with the evergreen hybrid groups first, and the deciduous hybrids next, followed by the species. Within each category, the least cold hardy groups are listed before the more cold hardy ones. The species azaleas are arranged with the native American species separate from the Asian ones.

Evergreen Azaleas

Name	Cold Hardiness	Flower Description	Plant Description	Bloom Season
BELGIAN INDICA				
'Albert and Elizabeth'	20°F	White with salmon-pink edges, double, 2 in. across.	Grows less than 3 ft tall.	Midseason
'Blushing Bride'	20°F	Blush-pink, double.	Grows less than 3 ft tall.	Late season
'Chimes'	20°F	Bell-shaped, rich red, semidouble.	Grows less than 3 ft tall.	Winter through spring
'Jean Haerens'	20°F	Frilled, deep rose-pink, double.	Grows less than 3 ft tall.	Early season
'Red Poppy'	20°F	Dark red, single.	Grows 3-6 ft tall.	Midseason
RUTHERFORDIANA				
'Alaska'	20°F	White with chartreuse blotch, single, some semi-double, 2 in. diameter.	Grows less than 3 ft tall.	Mid- to late season
'Dorothy Gish'	20°F	Frilled, single, orange-red, hose-in-hose, 2-1/2 in. across.	Grows less than 3 ft tall.	Mid- to late season
'Gloria'	20°F	Salmon-and-white variegated, hose-in-hose.	Grows 3 to 6 ft tall.	Early to midseason
'Pink Ruffles'	20°F	Shell-pink, double, 2 in. across.	Grows 3-5 ft tall.	Midseason
'Redwing'	20°F	Red, hose-in-hose, 3 in. across.	Grows less than 6 ft tall.	Midseason
SOUTHERN INDICA				
'Brilliant'	20°F	Red, single, 2-1/4 in. across.	Dense, spreading. Grows 3-5 ft tall.	Mid- to late season
'Coccinea Major'	20°F	Orange-red, single.	Spreading, dense, less than 3 ft tall.	Late
'Duc de Rohan'	20°F	Orange-red, single, 2-1/4 in. across.	Spreading. Grows 3-5 ft tall.	Early to midseason
'Fielder's White'	20°F	Frilled, white with chartreuse blotch, single, 2-3/4 in. across.	Spreading. Grows 3-5 ft tall.	Early to midseason
'Formosa'	20°F	Lavender-magenta, single, 3-1/2 in. across.	Upright. Grows to 6 ft tall or more.	Mid- to late season
'George Lindley Taber'	20°F	White, flushed violet-red with a darker blotch, single, 3-1/2 in. across.	Grows 3-5 ft tall.	Mid- to late season
'Glory of Sunninghill'	20°F	Orange-red, single, 2 in. across.	Dense, spreading. Grows 3-5 ft tall.	Late season
'Pride of Dorking'	20°F	Brilliant orange-red, single.	Grows less than 6 ft tall.	Late season
'Pride of Mobile' ('Elegans Superba')	20°F	Deep rose-pink, single 2-1/2 in. across.	Grows to 6 ft tall or more.	Mid- to late season
'Southern Charm'	20°F	A pink sport of 'Formosa', single, 3-1/3 in. across.	Grows to 6 ft tall or more.	Midseason

Deciduous Knap Hill/Exbury Hybrids make superb landscape specimen plants, adding glorious flower color to the garden in spring.

Name	Cold Hardiness	Flower Description	Plant Description	Bloom Season
GLENN DALE				
'Copperman'	5°F	Brilliant orange-red, single with overlapping lobes, 3 in. across.	Spreading, dense. Grows 3-5 ft tall.	Late
'Delaware Valley White'	5°F	Fragrant, white, single, 3 in. across.	Grows less than 6 ft tall.	Late season
'Everest'	5°F	White with chartreuse blotch, single, 2 in. across.	Grows 3-5 ft tall.	Late midseason
'Fashion'	5°F	Orange-red with red blotch, single, hose-in-hose, 2 in. across.	Grows more than 5 ft tall.	Early to midseason
'Gaiety'	5°F	Rose-pink with a darker blotch, single, 3 in. across.	Dark green narrow leaves. Grows 3-5 ft tall.	Late midseason
'Geisha'	5°F	White, flecked and striped purple, single, 1-1/2 to 2 in. across.	Grows less than 6 ft tall.	Very early season
'Glacier'	5°F	White with a chartreuse throat, single, 2-1/2 in. across.	Upright. Grows 3-5 ft tall.	Early to midseason
'Glamour'	0°F	Rose-red, single, 2-1/2 in. across.	Dark green leaves turn bronze in fall. Grows 3-5 ft tall.	Early to midseason
'Helen Close'	5°F	White with a pale yellow blotch, single, 2-1/2 to 3 in. across.	Spreading, dense. Grows 3-5 ft tall.	Midseason
'Martha Hitchcock'	5°F	White with magenta-pink margins, single, 3-1/2 in. across.	Grows 3-5 ft tall.	Late midseason
'Treasure'	5°F	White with pink blotch, single, 4 in. across.	Dark green leaves. Grows 3-5 ft tall.	Early to midseason
KURUME				
'Christmas Cheer'	5°F	Brilliant red, hose-in-hose, 1-1/4 in. across, in a tight truss.	Spreading. Grows 3-5 ft tall.	Early to midseason
'Coral Bells'	5°F	Shell-pink, single, hose-in-hose, tubular, 1-1/8 in. across.	Spreading. Grows less than 3 ft tall.	Early to midseason
'Eureka'	5°F	Pink, hose-in-hose.	Spreading. Grows less than 6 ft tall.	Late season
'Hershey's Red'	5°F	Bright red, double.	Grows less than 3 ft tall.	Midseason
'Hexe'	5°F	Crimson-red, hose-in-hose.	Grows 3-5 ft tall.	Mid- to late season
'H.H. Hume'	5°F	White, single, hose-in-hose, 2 in. across.	Spreading. Grows less than 6 ft tall.	Midseason
'Hino-Crimson'	5°F	Crimson-red, single.	Grows 3-5 ft tall.	Midseason
'Hinodegiri'	5°F	Violet rose-red, single, 1-1/2 in. across.	Compact. Grows 3-5 ft tall.	Early to midseason
'Orange Cup'	5°F	Reddish-orange, hose-in-hose.	Grows less than 6 ft tall.	Late season
'Pink Pearl'	5°F	Salmon-rose, hose-in-hose.	Upright. May grow to 6 ft or taller.	Midseason
'Sherwood Orchid'	5°F	Violet-red with a dark blotch, single.	Spreading. Grows 3-5 ft tall.	Midseason
'Sherwood Red'	5°F	Orange-red, single.	Grows 3-5 ft tall.	Early to midseason
'Snow'	5°F	White, hose-in-hose, 1-1/2 in. across.	Upright, spreading. Grows less than 6 ft tall.	Midseason
'Vuyk's Scarlet'	5°F	Bright scarlet, single, very large.	Grows less than 6 ft tall.	Midseason
PERICAT				
'Sweetheart Supreme'	5°F	Frilled rose-pink with a dark blotch, semidouble, hose-in-hose, 1-3/4 in. across.	Dense and spreading. Grows 3-5 ft tall.	Mid- to late season

Mass plantings of azaleas can be planned to provide a continuous floral display from early spring into summer.

Name	Cold Hardiness	Flower Description	Plant Description	Bloom Season
SATSUKI/MACRANTHA				
'Beni-Kirishima'	5°F	Orange-red with a darker blotch, double, 2 in. across.	Grows 3-5 ft tall.	Late season
'Chinzan'	5°F	Light salmon-pink, single, large.	Compact, excellent for bonsai use with flexible branches. Grows less than 3 ft tall.	Late season
'Flame Creeper'	5°F	Orange-red, single.	Creeping plant with small leaves. Good ground cover. Grows less than 3 ft tall.	Late season
'Gumpo Pink'	5°F	Light pink, single, large.	Dense. Grows less than 3 ft tall.	Late season
'Gumpo White'	5°F	White with occasional red flakes, single, 3 in. across.	Low-growing, with small leaves. Grows less than 3 ft tall.	Late season
'Linda R.'	5°F	Soft, solid pastel-pink, single.	Dense. Grows less than 3 ft tall.	Midseason
'Salmon Macrantha'	5°F	Salmon-pink to purple, single.	Grows less than 3 ft tall.	Mid- to late season.
GABLE				
'Campfire'	0°F	Flame-red with a darker blotch, hose-in-hose.	Dense. Grows less than 6 ft tall.	Midseason
'Caroline Gable'	0°F	Red, hose-in-hose, 1-3/4 in. across.	Grows less than 6 ft tall.	Midseason
'Kathy'	0°F	Frilled, white, single.	Grows less than 3 ft tall.	Mid- to late season
'Lorna'	0°F	Pastel-pink, double, hose-in-hose, 1-3/4 in. across.	Spreading. Grows less than 3 ft tall.	Late season
'Purple Splendor'	0°F	Ruffled, lavender with a dark blotch, hose-in-hose.	Grows less than 6 ft tall.	Midseason
'Rosebud'	0°F	Violet-red, double, hose-in-hose, 1-3/4 in. across.	Low, dense, spreading. Grows slowly up to 3 ft tall.	Late season
'Rose Greeley'	0°F	Fragrant, white with chartreuse blotch, single, hose-in-hose, 2-1/2 in. across.	Dense, spreading. Grows less than 3 ft tall.	Early to midseason
'Stewartstonian'	0°F	Bright, clear red, single.	Upright, compact, bushy. Winter foliage wine-red. Ideal for bonsai. Grows to 6-8 ft.	Late season
GIRARD				
'Girard Crimson'	– 5°F	Crimson, single.	Grows less than 6 ft tall.	Midseason
'Girard Pink'	– 5°F	Pink, single.	Grows less than 3 ft tall.	Late season
'Hot Shot'	– 5°F	Orange-red, double.	Grows 3-5 ft tall.	Mid- to late season
'Rene Michelle'	– 5°F	Pink, single, with heavy substance.	Grows less than 3 ft tall.	Midseason
'Roberta'	– 5°F	Pink, double.	Grows less than 6 ft tall.	Midseason
KAEMPFERI				
'Alice'	– 10°F	Salmon-red, fading to pale rose.	Grows to 6 ft tall or more.	Early to mid-season
'Fedora'	– 10°F	Violet-red or phlox-pink, single, 2 in. across.	Upright. Grows to 6 ft tall or more.	Early season
'Herbert'	– 10°F	Reddish-violet, hose-in-hose.	Spreading. Grows less than 6 ft tall.	Midseason
'Palestrina' ('Wilhelmina Vuyk')	– 10°F	White with chartreuse blotch, single, 2-1/4 in. across.	Grows 3-5 ft tall.	Mid- to late season

'Toucan' (Knap Hill/Exbury Hybrid)

Smooth azalea *(R. arborescens)*

Deciduous Azaleas
KNAP HILL/EXBURY HYBRIDS

Name	Cold Hardiness	Flower Description	Plant Description	Bloom Season
'Aurora'	−20°F	Pale salmon-pink with an orange blotch.	Grows less than 6 ft tall.	Midseason
'Balzac'	−20°F	Star-shaped, very fragrant, red-orange with flame markings on upper petals, in trusses.	Grows less than 6 ft tall.	Late
'Brazil'	−20°F	Small, frilled, showy tangerine-red. Blooms in profusion.	Grows less than 6 ft tall.	Late
'Cecile'	−20°F	Very large, salmon-pink with a yellow blotch.	Grows less than 6 ft tall.	Late
'Fireball'	−20°F	Deep fiery-red.	Grows less than 6 ft tall.	Midseason
'Gibraltar'	−20°F	Bright orange-red with cherry coloring, in tight ball-shaped trusses.	Compact growth. Grows less than 6 ft tall.	Midseason
'Gold Dust'	−20°F	Solid gold, in ball-like trusses.	Grows less than 6 ft tall.	Midseason
'Klondyke'	−20°F	Orange-yellow bells open to flowers of solid deep tangerine-yellow.	Grows less than 6 ft tall.	Late
'Royal Lodge'	−20°F	Dark red with long stamens.	Dark, reddish-brown foliage. Grows less than 6 ft tall.	Very late
'Toucan'	−20°F	Light creamy-yellow with margins tinged pink.	Grows less than 6 ft tall.	Mid- to late season

MOLLIS HYBRIDS

Name	Cold Hardiness	Flower Description	Plant Description	Bloom Season
'Christopher Wren'	−20°F	Large, yellow with a tangerine blotch.	Grows more than 6 ft tall.	Mid- to late season
'Directeur Moerlands'	−20°F	Sunset-gold with a darker blotch.	Grows more than 6 ft tall.	Mid- to late season
'Koster's Brilliant Red'	−20°F	Orange-red. Single.	Grows more than 6 ft tall.	Mid- to late season

OCCIDENTALE HYDRIDS

Name	Cold Hardiness	Flower Description	Plant Description	Bloom Season
'Graciosa'	−25°F	Slightly frilled, pale yellow flushed rose.	Grows to 5-6 ft tall.	Early to midseason
'Irene Koster'	−25°F	Pure rose-pink with a small yellow blotch.	Grows to 5-6 ft tall.	Early to midseason
'Westminster'	−20°F	Clear almond-pink flowers.	Grows less than 6 ft tall.	Early

GHENT HYBRIDS

Name	Cold Hardiness	Flower Description	Plant Description	Bloom Season
'Coccinea Speciosa'	−25°F	Brilliant orange-red with a yellowish-orange blotch.	Grows to 5-6 ft tall.	Early to midseason
'Daviesii'	−25°F	Very pale yellow fading to almost white with a showy yellow blotch, 2-1/4 in. across.	Grows more than 6 ft tall.	Late
'Narcissiflora'	−25°F	Fragrant, double yellow.	Grows more than 6 ft tall.	Late

Asian Native Azaleas

Botanical Name/ Common Name	Cold Hardiness	Origin	Flower Description	Plant Description	Bloom Season	Comments
R. japonicum Japanese Azalea	−25°F	Japan	Varies from yellow to orange to red, 2 in. across.	Dense, 2-6 ft tall. Deciduous.	Midseason	One of the parents of Mollis and Exbury hybrids.
R. luteum (R. flavum) Pontic Azalea	−25°F	Caucacus of E. Europe	Very fragrant, bright sunny yellow-orange, 2 in. across.	Grows to 2-12 ft tall. Deciduous. Fall color.	Midseason	One of parents of Ghent hybrids.
R. molle (R. mollis) Chinese Azalea	−20°F	China	Yellow to yellow-orange, spotted green, 2 in. across.	Dense, 4 ft tall. Deciduous.	Early to midseason	One of parents of Mollis and Exbury hybrids.
R. obtusum kaempferi (R. kaempferi)	−10°F	Asian	Slightly frilled, salmon-pink to salmon-orange.	Semievergreen to deciduous. Under 6 ft tall.	Mid- to late season	Prime parent of Kaempferi hybrids.
R. schlippenbachii Royal Azalea	−25°F	Manchuria, Korea, Japan	Large, fragrant, pink or rose-pink, brown-dotted throats, 2-3 in. across.	Grows to 4 ft tall or more. Dense. Deciduous. Brilliant fall foliage.	Early to mid-season, as leaves open.	Give partial shade. Beautiful but fastidious.
R. yedoense poukhanense Korean Azalea	− 5°F	Korea, Japan	Fragrant, rosy-lilac, 2 in. across.	Grows to 4-6 ft tall. Deciduous.	Early to midseason	May be semievergreen. One of the parents of Gable hybrids.

North American Native Azaleas

Botanical Name/ Common Name	Cold Hardiness	Origin	Flower Description	Plant Description	Bloom Season	Comments
R. arborescens Smooth Azalea, Sweet Azalea,	−20°F	N.Y. and Pa., south to mt. tops of Ga. and Ala.	Fragrant, pure white with pink or reddish flush and yellow blotch on upper petal, 2 in. across. Long stamens.	Reaches 6-10 ft tall. Deciduous.	Mid- to late season	A parent of Exbury hybrids.
R. atlanticum Coast Azalea	−10°F	Coastal Plains, Del. south to S. Car., Ga.	Fragrant, white or white flushed with pale red, some with yellow blotch, 1-3/4 in. long.	Low-growing shrub, 1-2 ft tall. Spreading roots. Deciduous.	Midseason	Flowers appear before leaves.
R. austrinum Florida Flame Azalea	−10°F	Fla., Ga., and Ala.	Fragrant, golden-yellow, 1-1/4 in. long.	Reaches 10-12 ft tall. Deciduous.	Very early.	Flowers appear before or with leaves.
R. bakeri Cumberland Azalea	−20°F	High elevations of W. Va., Ky., Tenn., south to Ga., Ala.	May be orange, red, or yellow with gold blotch, 1-1/2- to 2-in. across.	Varies from 1-10 ft tall. Deciduous.	Mid- to late season	Flowers appear after leaves.
R. calendulaceum Flame Azalea	−20°F	Appalachian Mts., N. Pa., Ohio, south to N. Ga.	Orange-red to clear yellow, 2-in. diameter.	Varies from 4-10 ft tall, rarely 15 ft tall. Deciduous.	Mid- to late season	Claimed as one of the most beautiful native shrubs. A parent of Exbury hybrids.
R. canadense Rhodora	−40°F	East coast of Labrador, south to N.J.	Bell-shaped with short tubes, 2 lips, 3/4 in. across. Rose-purple to white.	Grows to 3-4 ft tall. Dense. Deciduous.	Early to midseason	Flowers appear before leaves.
R. canescens Piedmont or Florida Pinxter Azalea	0°F	N.C., Tenn., south to Tx., Ala., Ga., N. Fla.	Fragrant, varying from white to light or deep pink, 1-1/2 in. across. Long stamens.	Reaches 10-15 ft tall. Deciduous.	Early to midseason	Flowers appear before or with leaves.
R. occidentale Western Azalea	− 5°F	S. Ore., south to S. Calif.	Fragrant, white to pinkish, splashed yellow or pink, often with a rosy throat. 2-1/2 in. across.	Grows to 6-10 ft tall and as wide. Deciduous.	Mid- to late season	Difficult to grow in the East. Used in development of Ghent and Exbury hybrids.
R. periclymenoides (R. nudiflorum) Pinxterbloom Azalea	−30°F	Mass., south to Ohio, N.C., Tenn., and Ga.	Sweet, fragrant, varying from white or pale pink to deep violet, 1-1/2 in. across.	Grows to 4-6 ft tall, rarely to 10 ft. Deciduous.	Early season	Used in breeding Ghent hybrids. One of the most common native azaleas.
R. prinophyllum Rose-Shell Azalea	−30°F	New England, south to mts. of Va., west to Mo.	Spicy, clove-scented, rose-pink to deep pink, 1-1/2 in. across.	Grows to 2-9 ft tall, rarely to 15 ft. Deciduous.	Midseason	Flowers appear with leaves.
R. prunifolium Plum-Leaved or Prunifolia Azalea	−10°F	S. W. Ga. and eastern Ala., along streams.	Varies from apricot to pale orange, orange-red to red, 1-1/2 in. across.	Reaches 8-15 ft tall. Deciduous.	Late to very late	Unusual candy-striped flowers buds.
R. serrulatum Hammock-Sweet Azalea	0°F	Wooded swamps of E. Ga., Fla., west to La.	Fragrance of cloves, white to creamy-white, 1-1/2 in. long. Long stamens.	Toothed leaves and red-brown twigs. Reaches 20 ft tall. Deciduous.	Very late	Flowers appear after leaves. Grows in wet soil. Valuable in South for very late bloom.
R. vaseyi Pink-Shell Azalea	−30°F	Mts. of west N. C., above 3,000 ft.	Bell-shaped, green-throated, rose-pink, with orange-red dots. 1-1/2 in. across.	Reaches 12-15 ft tall. Deciduous	Early to midseason	Flowers appear before leaves.
R. viscosum Swamp Azalea	−30°F	Swamps from Maine south to Ala., Ga.	Slender, small-tubed, 2 in. long, white to creamy-white or pale pink; spicy scent.	Grows to 8 ft tall. Deciduous.	Mid- to late season	Spreads by underground runners. Grows in wet soil. Parent of Exbury hybrids.

'Pink Ruffles' (Rutherfordiana Hybrid)

'Delaware Valley White' (Glenn Dale Hybrid)

'Redwing' (Rutherfordiana Hybrid)

Evergreen Azaleas by Color

White

'Alaska' . . . . Rutherfordiana
'Albert and Elizabeth' (with pink margins)
. . . . Belgian Indica
'Delaware Valley White' . . . . Glenn Dale
'Everest' . . . . Glenn Dale
'Fielder's White' . . . . Southern Indica
'Geisha' . . . . Glenn Dale
'George Lindley Taber' . Southern Indica
'Glacier' . . . . Glenn Dale
'Gumpo White' . . . . . Satsuki/Macrantha
'H.H. Hume' . . . . Kurume
'Helen Close' . . . . Glenn Dale
'Kathy' . . . . Gable
'Martha Hitchcock' (with lavender
markings) . . . . Glenn Dale
'Palestrina' . . . . Kaempferi
'Rose Greeley' . . . . Gable
'Snow' . . . . Kurume
'Treasure' . . . . Glenn Dale

Pink

'Blushing Bride' . . . . Belgian Indica
'Chinzan' . . . . Satsuki/Macrantha
'Coral Bells' . . . . Kurume
'Eureka' . . . . Kurume
'Fedora' . . . . Kaempferi
'Gaiety' . . . . Glenn Dale
'Girard Pink' . . . . Girard
'Gloria' . . . . Rutherfordiana
'Gumpo Pink' . . . . . . Satsuki/Macrantha
'Jean Haerens' . . . . Belgian Indica
'Linda R.' . . . . Satsuki/Macrantha
'Lorna' . . . . Gable
R. obtusum kaempferi . . . Asian species
'Pink Pearl' . . . . Kurume
'Pink Ruffles' . . . . Rutherfordiana
'Pride of Mobile' . . . . Southern Indica
'Rene Michele' . . . . Girard
'Roberta' . . . . Girard
'Salmon Macrantha' .Satsuki/Macrantha
'Southern Charm' . . . . . Southern Indica
'Sweetheart Supreme' . . . . Pericat

Orange-Red

'Alice' . . . . Kaempferi
'Beni-Kirishima' . . . . Satsuki/Macrantha
'Coccinea' . . . . Southern Indica
'Copperman' . . . . Glenn Dale
'Dorothy Gish' . . . . Rutherfordiana
'Duc de Rohan' . . . . Southern Indica
'Fashion' . . . . Glenn Dale
'Flame Creeper' . . . . Satsuki/Macrantha
'Glory of Sunninghill' . . . Southern Indica
'Hotshot' . . . . Girard
'Orange Cup' . . . . Kurume
'Pride of Dorking' . . . . . . Southern Indica
'Sherwood Red' . . . . Kurume

Purple to Lavender

'Formosa' . . . . Southern Indica
'Purple Splendor' . . . . Gable

Violet-Red to Crimson

'Fedora' . . . . Kaempferi
'Girard Crimson' . . . . Girard
'Glamour' . . . . Glenn Dale
'Herbert' . . . . Kaempferi
'Hexe' . . . . Kurume
'Hino-Crimson' . . . . Kurume
'Hinodegiri' . . . . Kurume
'Rosebud' . . . . Gable
'Sherwood Orchid' . . . . Kurume

Red

'Brilliant' . . . . Southern Indica
'Campfire' . . . . Gable
'Caroline Gable' . . . . Gable
'Chimes' . . . . Belgian Indica
'Christmas Cheer' . . . . Kurume
'Hershey's Red' . . . . Kurume
'Red Poppy' . . . . Belgian Indica
'Redwing' . . . . Rutherfordiana
'Stewartstonian' . . . . Gable
'Vuyk's Scarlet' . . . . Kurume

Deciduous Azaleas by Color

White
R. arborescens	American species
R. atlanticum	American species
R. canescens	American species
'Daviesii'	Ghent
R. occidentale	American species
R. serrulatum	American species
R. viscosum	American species

Pink
'Aurora'	Knap Hill/Exbury
'Cecile'	Knap Hill/Exbury
'Irene Koster'	Occidentale
R. mucronulatum	Asian species
R. periclymenoides	American species
R. prinophyllum	American species
R. schlippenbachii	Asian species
R. vaseyi	American species
'Westminster'	Occidentale

Orange to Red
R. bakeri	American species
'Balzac'	Knap Hill/Exbury
'Brazil'	Knap Hill/Exbury
R. calendulaceum	American species
'Coccinea Speciosa'	Ghent
'Fireball'	Knap Hill/Exbury
'Gibraltar'	Knap Hill/Exbury
R. japonicum	Asian species
'Koster's Brilliant Red'	Mollis
R. obtusum kaempferi	Asian Species
R. prunifolium	American species
'Royal Lodge'	Knap Hill/Exbury

Yellow
R. austrinum	American species
R. calendulaceum	American species
'Christopher Wren'	Mollis
'Directeur Moerlands'	Mollis
'Gold Dust'	Knap Hill/Exbury
'Graciosa'	Occidentale
'Klondyke'	Knap Hill/Exbury
R. luteum	Asian species
R. molle	Asian species
'Narcissiflora'	Ghent
'Toucan'	Knap Hill/Exbury

Purple
R. canadense	American species
R. yedoense poukhanense	Asian species

Deciduous azaleas have a delicate graceful appearance. They provide a color show in spring when they blossom and again in fall when the foliage takes on brilliant hues.

Pink-shell azalea *(R. vaseyi),* a deciduous native American species, bears delicate long tubular flowers before leaves emerge.

Top-Rated Rhododendrons

Grand and majestic, with whorls of large leathery blue-green leaves and bouquets of elegant flowers, rhododendrons are prized shrubs wherever they are grown. There are thousands of named varieties, making selecting ones for your garden a seemingly difficult task. The lists that follow help make the selecting easy. They describe top-rated rhododendrons—those chosen by experienced horticulturists for their beauty, ease of care, and availability.

The lists describe the flower clusters, which are called "trusses". Trusses may be loose, compact, ball-shaped, dome-shaped, cervical (elongated), or bell-like. The lists also describe leaf size and color and plant height and density. Rhododendrons with small leaves are generally considered more sun-tolerant than large-leaved kinds. Use the notations on bloom season to select late-blooming plants for borderline hardy areas and to select plants that bloom at different times.

ARS RATINGS

Each rhododendron is rated by the American Rhododendron Society (ARS) on flower and plant quality. A scale of 1 to 5 is used, with 1 being poor and 5 being superior. For example, 'Boule de Neige' is rated 4/4. The first number means that the flower is considered above average; the second number means that the plant form and foliage are also considered above average.

These ratings should not be used as the ultimate test of plant usefulness. If you live in a region where rhododendrons are a bit finicky, you might prefer to choose ones that are rated slightly lower but are more cold hardy.

At left: 'Anah Kruschke' rhododendron bears long showy trusses of rich purple flowers late in the season; has lush dense foliage.

'Unique' rhododendron

'Nova Zembla' rhododendron

'Catawbiense Album' rhododendron

'Lee's Dark Purple' rhododendron

'Catawbiense Album' rhododendron

'Lee's Dark Purple' rhododendron

Rhododendrons

Name	Cold Hardiness	Flower Description	Plant Description	Bloom Season	Ratings & Comments
'Arthur Bedford'	− 5°F	Lavender-blue with a distinctive dark blotch. Dome-shaped trusses.	Grows vigorously to 6 ft tall.	Mid- to late season	4/3. Tolerates full sun.
'America'	−20°F	Bright red flowers in tight, ball-shaped trusses.	Sprawling habit, to 5 ft tall.	Midseason	3/3. Popular ironclad.
'Anah Kruschke'	−10°F	Lavender-purple held in medium-large, tight, elongated trusses.	Bushy, to 6 ft tall. Dense, lush foliage.	Late season	4/4. Withstands full sun.
'Anna Rose Whitney'	− 5°F	Large, rose-pink, in trusses of 12 flowers.	Grows to 6 ft tall. Dense foliage.	Mid- to late season	4/4. Well-shaped.
'Antoon van Welie'	− 5°F	Deep pink, in big trusses.	Compact, vigorous grower reaching 6 ft tall. Broad, waxy, 6-in.-long leaves.	Mid- to late season	4/4.
'Blue Ensign'	−10°F	Lilac to lavender-blue with a purplish-black blotch, frilled, held in rounded trusses.	Grows to 4 ft tall, upright and spreading with glossy dark leaves.	Midseason	4/4. Tolerates full sun.
'Blue Jay'	− 5°F	Lavender-blue blotched with brown, in compact, elongated trusses.	Grows vigorously to 5 ft tall with large, bright green leaves.	Mid- to late season	3/4.
'Blue Peter'	−10°F	Light lavender-blue with a purple blotch, frilled, in elongated trusses.	Grows to 4-5 ft tall with glossy leaves.	Midseason	4/3. Popular on East Coast.
'Boule de Neige'	−25°F	Trusses of white flowers resemble snowballs.	Compact shrub grows to 5 ft tall with bright green leathery leaves.	Midseason	4/4. Tolerates heat, sun and extreme cold.
'Bow Bells'	0°F	Deep pink buds open to light pink cup-shaped flowers in loose trusses.	Rounded, spreading growth habit, eventually reaching 3 ft tall.	Early to midseason	3/4. Leaves appear after flowers, emerging shiny copper color, maturing to medium green.
'Bric-a-Brac'	5°F	Trusses display flowers that open to shades of white or pink, with chocolate-brown anthers.	Low-growing, reaching 30 in. tall.	Very early	4/3. Leaves fuzzy, round, dark green.
'Caractacus'	−25°F	Purplish-red.	Compact shrub, to 6 ft tall.	Late season	2/3. Requires partial shade.
'Carmen'	− 5°F	Lavender to dark red.	Dwarf, grows slowly to 1 ft tall with round, emerald-green leaves.	Early to midseason	4/5. Handsome when not in bloom.
'Caroline'	−15°F	Fragrant, orchid-pink.	Grows to 6 ft tall. Leaves waxy with wavy margins.	Mid- to late season	3/4. Long-lasting flowers.
R. carolinianum	−25°F	Pure white to pale rose, rose, lilac-rose, or commonly light purple-rose.	Compact, grows 4 ft tall.	Midseason	3/3. Native of Blue Ridge Mountains of the Carolinas and Tenn. R. carolinianum album is favored by many.
R. catawbiense	−25°F	Lilac-purple, sometimes purple-rose, spotted with green or brown-yellow. Trusses of 15 to 20 flowers.	Grows to 6 ft tall. Leaves medium-large, smooth, shiny dark green on top, pale green below.	Mid- to late season	2/2. Native to slopes and summits of southern Alleghenys, W. Va. south to Ga. and Ala. One of hardiest and best-known species.
'Catawbiense Album'	−25°F	Pure white spotted with greenish yellow, in rounded trusses.	Compact, spreading, grows to 6 ft tall. Slightly convex dark green leaves.	Late season	3/3. Deserves to be called an ironclad.

Many rhododendrons make fine specimen plants. Their foliage and form are attractive year-round. During their bloom season their magnificent flower color is incomparable.

Name	Cold Hardiness	Flower Description	Plant Description	Bloom Season	Ratings & Comments
'Chionoides'	−15°F	Bright white, in numerous trusses.	Compact, grows to 4-6 ft tall.	Mid- to late season	3/4. Very easy to grow.
R. chryseum (R. rupicola chryseum)	−15°F	Bell-shaped, bright yellow, in clusters.	Dwarf, grows to 12 in. tall. Leaves 1/2 to 1 in. long.	Early to midseason	4/3. Many dense branches.
'Cunningham's White'	−10°F	Small, white with greenish-yellow blotch in small, upright trusses.	Semidwarf, compact, spreading to 4 ft wide with shiny, dark leaves.	Mid- to late season	2/3. Requires partial shade.
'Daphnoides'	−10°F	Bright purple, displayed in pomponlike trusses.	Grows to 4 ft tall forming dense mound.	Mid- to late season	3/4. Foliage unique, with tightly spaced, rolled glossy leaves.
'Dr. V.H. Rutgers'	−20°F	Frilled, crimson-red.	Grows to 5 ft tall.	Mid- to late season	3/3. Dense foliage with dark green leaves.
'Dora Amateis'	−15°F	Spicy-scented, 2 in. across, pure white with green spots, in clusters of up to 5.	Semidwarf, grows to 3 ft tall with dense foliage.	Early to midseason	4/4. Leaves tinged bronze when grown in full sun.
'English Roseum'	−20°F	Rose-pink, tinged lavender, in big trusses.	Grows to 6 ft tall or more.	Mid- to late season	2/4. Handsome plant, even when not in bloom. Tolerates extreme heat, cold, and humidity.
R. fastigiatum	−15°F	Lilac-purple, in small clusters that cover foliage.	Reaches 18 in. with dense, dark, shiny foliage.	Midseason	4/4. One of the hardiest of small alpine-type rhododendrons.
'Fastuosum Flore Pleno'	−10°F	Lavender-purple, double, 2 in. across, held in full trusses.	Grows vigorously to 6 ft tall with leaves dark above, light green below.	Mid- to late season	3/3. Open and rounded growth habit.
'Fragrantissimum'	20°F	Funnel-shaped, white tinged with pink, very fragrant.	Generally seen as espalier or vine to 10 ft or more. Can be kept to 5-6 ft or less with pruning.	Midseason	4/3. Flowers nutmeg-scented.
'General Eisenhower'	5°F	Large, ruffled, deep carmine-red in large clusters.	Compact, grows to 6 ft tall with large, waxy leaves.	Midseason	4/3. Strong-growing plant.
'Gomer Waterer'	−15°F	Pink flower buds open to pure white.	Grows to 5 ft tall with large, dark leaves.	Mid- to late season	3/5. Old standby tolerates full sun.
'Graf Zeppelin'	10°F	Vibrant bright pink.	Grows to 5 ft tall with dark, glossy leaves.	Mid- to late season	3/4. Vigorous and hardy.
'Herbert Parsons' ('President Lincoln')	−25°F	Lavender-pink.	Grows to 6 ft tall or more.	Mid- to late season	2/3.
'Humming Bird'	0°F	Red flowers hold their color well.	Semidwarf shrub with compact habit reaches 2-1/2 ft tall.	Early to midseason	3/4. Requires partial shade.
'Ignatius Sargent'	−20°F	Large, rose-red, slightly fragrant.	Grows to 5-6 ft tall with large leaves.	Mid- to late season	2/2. Plant has open growth habit.
R. impeditum	−15°F	Small, slightly fragrant, bright purplish-blue flowers blanket foliage.	Tight, compact, cushionlike dwarf shrub reaches 1-1/2 ft high. Tiny silvery gray-green leaves.	Midseason	4/4. Excellent for bonsai.
R. intricatum	−15°F	Attractive bluish flowers in profusion.	Low, compact, intricately branched shrub reaches 1-2 ft tall.	Early to midseason	4/3. Ideal for bonsai.

The flowers of many rhododendrons are distinguished with contrasting markings, such as the bold black blotch on the white petals of 'Sappho'.

Rhododendrons

Name	Cold Hardiness	Flower Description	Plant Description	Bloom Season	Ratings & Comments
'Janet Blair'	−15°F	Frilled, light pink with a green flare on the upper petals.	Grows vigorously to 6 ft tall.	Midseason	4/3. Profuse foliage.
R. keiskei	− 5°F	Lemon-yellow, bell-shaped, in clusters.	Grows to 3 ft tall. Variety *cordifolia* is dwarf, to 6 in.	Early to midseason	4/4. Very pointed leaves.
R. keleticum	−10°F	Large, pansylike, standing erect above foliage, ranging from rose through purple with crimson flecks.	Dwarf, reaching 1 ft tall, with dense, aromatic leaves.	Midseason	4/4. Good choice for bonsai.
'Kluis Sensation'	0°F	Dark red in tight trusses.	Compact shrub to 5 ft tall.	Mid- to late season	3/4. Dark red flowers contrast with dark green leaves.
'Lee's Dark Purple'	−20°F	Dark purple, in large trusses.	Grows to 6 ft tall with dark, wavy foliage.	Mid- to late season	3/3. Ironclad. Popular old-timer.
R. maximum	−25°F	White petals, rose or pink flushed. Trusses partially hidden by current season's leaf growth.	Grows from 4-ft-tall shrub to 40-ft-tall tree, depending on climate.	Mid- to late season	2/3. Leaves resemble a bay tree.
'Moonstone'	0°F	Bell-shaped, creamy-yellow, in trusses of 3 to 5.	Grows in a tight mound, 3 ft tall, covered with smooth oval-shaped green leaves 2-1/2 in. long.	Early to midseason	4/4. Prolific bloomer.
'Mother of Pearl'	0°F	Buds open pink, fade to pearl-white. Slightly fragrant.	Grows rapidly to 6 ft tall.	Midseason	4/3. A sport of 'Pink Pearl'.
R. moupinense	− 5°F	Funnel-shaped, large, fragrant, bright snowy-white with a maroon blotch.	Open, spreading growth to 30 in. wide. Bronzy-red new growth matures to shiny green leaves.	Very early season	4/3. Good choice for bonsai.
'Mrs. Charles E. Pearson'	− 5°F	Large, light orchid-pink with upper petals spotted brown, in dome-shaped trusses.	Grows vigorously to 6 ft tall with lush foliage.	Midseason	4/4. Award-winning old-timer. Vigorous. Tolerates sun and heat.
'Mrs. Furnival'	−10°F	Light pink with a striking brown blotch on the upper petals, in tight, dome-shaped trusses.	Upright, spreading, reaching 4 ft tall with light green leaves.	Mid- to late season	5/4. Grows well in eastern United States.
R. mucronulatum	−15°F	Orchid-pink blossoms 1-3/4 in. across appear before leaves. 'Cornell Pink' is rose-colored.	Grows to 5-8 ft tall. Red fall color.	Very early	ARS rating not available. Deciduous. Botanists consider this azalea-like shrub a rhododendron.
'Nova Zembla'	−25°F	Dark red, showy, in rounded trusses.	Grows to 5 ft tall with polished, dark green leaves.	Midseason	3/3. Grows well in difficult areas.
'Parson's Gloriosum'	−25°F	Lavender-pink in conical trusses.	Grows compact, upright, to 5 ft tall with dark green leaves.	Midseason	2/2. Very hardy. Ironclad.
R. pemakoense	0°F	Profusion of pink flowers hides leaves.	Dwarf, compact, cushionlike to 1-1/2 ft with tiny, 1-in.-long leaves.	Very early to early season	3/4. Very easy to grow.
'Pink Pearl'	− 5°F	Rose-pink in large trusses.	Tall, open growth to 6 ft.	Midseason	3/3.
'P.J.M.'	−20°F	Lavender-pink in small trusses.	Compact-growing to 4 ft tall with small leaves mahogany during winter.	Early season	4/4. Will withstand full sun as well as cold and heat.

'Unique' rhododendron

'Vulcan' rhododendron

Name	Cold Hardiness	Flower Description	Plant Description	Bloom Season	Ratings & Comments
'Purple Gem'	−20°F	Deep purple-violet.	Compact, spreading, grows to 2 ft with bluish-green foliage.	Early to midseason	3/4. Related to 'Ramapo'.
'Purple Splendor'	−10°F	Dark purple with a black blotch; appearing almost black overall.	Shrub grows to 5 ft with deep green foliage.	Mid- to late season	4/3. The king of royal purples.
'Ramapo'	−20°F	Pale violet, small, in profusion.	Dwarf, compact, spreading, reaches 2 ft. New leaves dusty blue.	Early to midseason	4/4. Use in low borders or rock gardens. Foliage is interesting throughout all seasons.
'Roseum Elegans'	−25°F	Small, rosy-lilac, held in dome-shaped trusses.	Grows vigorously to 6 ft with abundant olive-green foliage.	Mid- to late season	2/4. Another ironclad. Also for hot climates.
'Sappho'	−10°F	Medium-size, white with a blackish blotch on upper petals, in dome-shaped trusses.	Grows vigorously with open growth to 6 ft.	Midseason	3/2. Blooms profusely.
'Scarlet Wonder'	−10°F	Ruffled, scarlet-red, in flattened trusses.	Very compact, reaching 2 ft with dense, glossy leaves.	Midseason	5/4. Awarded silver and gold medal by Dutch enthusiasts.
'Scintillation'	−10°F	Pastel-pink, with a bronze and yellow throat, in large, dome-shaped trusses.	Grows to 5 ft with deep shiny green foliage.	Midseason	4/4. Wavy leaves curl attractively.
'The Hon. Jean Marie de Montague'	0°F	Bright red, showy, in rounded trusses.	Compact shrub grows to 5 ft tall with thick, heavy emerald-green foliage.	Midseason	4/4. Standard for excellence for red flowers.
'Trilby'	−10°F	Dark, crimson-red with black markings in the center, displayed in ball-like trusses.	Compact habit, reaches 5 ft with red stems, gray-green leaves.	Mid- to late season	3/4. Handsome plant, even when not in bloom.
'Unique'	0°F	Buds open light pink, change to buttery cream-yellow flushed with peach. Displayed profusely on dome-shaped trusses.	Compact, neat, reaches 4 ft with thick, oblong clover-green leaves.	Early to midseason	4/4. Flowers completely cover plant.
'Vulcan'	−10°F	Bright fire-red.	Mound-shaped, grows to 5 ft tall.	Mid- to late season	4/4. An excellent hybrid.
'Windbeam'	−25°F	Open white, turning light pink.	Spreading, grows to 4 ft with small leaves.	Early to midseason	4/3. Aromatic foliage.
'Yaku King'	−10°F	Deep pink with light pink blotch. Up to 18 blossoms in a ball-like truss.	Semidwarf, grows less than 3 ft tall.	Mid- to late season	ARS rating not available.
'Yaku Prince'	−10°F	Pink blossom, lighter blotch with reddish-orange spots. Up to 14 blossoms in a ball-like truss.	Semidwarf, grows less than 3 ft tall.	Midseason	ARS rating not available.
'Yaku Princess'	−10°F	Apple-blossom pink with a blushed blotch, greenish spots. Up to 15 blossoms in a ball-like truss.	Semidwarf, grows less than 3 ft tall.	Midseason	ARS rating not available.
'Yaku Queen'	−10°F	Pale pink with a faint yellow blotch. Up to 16 blossoms in a ball-like truss.	Semidwarf, grows less than 3 ft tall.	Midseason	ARS rating not available.
R. yakusimanum	−15°F	Pale rose.	Semidwarf, grows less than 3 ft tall.	Midseason	5/5. Limited availability but very popular among hobbyists.

43

'Roseum Elegans' rhododendron   'Sappho' rhododendron   'Anah Kruschke' rhododendron

Rhododendrons by Color

Pink

	Recommended Zones
'Anna Rose Whitney'	7-8
'Antoon van Welie'	7-8
'Bow Bells'	7-8
'Bric-a-Brac'	8-9
'Caroline'	6-8
R. carolinianum	5-8
'English Roseum'	5-8
'Graf Zeppelin'	7-8
'Herbert Parsons'	5-8
'Janet Blair'	6-8
'Mrs. Charles E. Pearson'	7-8
'Mrs. Furnival'	6-8
R. mucronulatum	6-8
'Parson's Gloriosum'	5-8
R. pemakoense	7-8
'Pink Pearl'	7-8
'P.J.M.'	5-8
'Roseum Elegans'	5-8
'Scintillation'	6-8
'Yaku King'	6-8
'Yaku Prince'	6-8
'Yaku Princess'	6-8
'Yaku Queen'	6-8
R. yakusimanum	6-8

Red

	Recommended Zones
'America'	5-8
'Caractacus'	5-8
'Carmen'	7-8
'Dr. V.H. Rutgers'	5-8
'General Eisenhower'	7-8
'Humming Bird'	7-9
'Ignatius Sargent'	5-8
'Kluis Sensation'	7-8
'Nova Zembla'	5-8
'Scarlet Wonder'	6-8
'The Hon. Jean Marie de Montague'	7-8
'Trilby'	6-8
'Vulcan'	7-8

White

	Recommended Zones
'Boule de Neige'	5-8
'Bric-a-Brac'	8-9
R. carolinianum	5-8
'Catawbiense Album'	5-8
'Chionoides'	5-8
'Cunningham's White'	6-8
'Dora Amateis'	6-9
'Fragrantissimum'	9-10
'Gomer Waterer'	6-8
'Mother of Pearl'	7-9
R. maximum	5-8
R. moupinense	7-9
'Sappho'	7-8
'Windbeam'	5-8

Yellow

	Recommended Zones
R. chryseum	6-7
R. keiskei	7-8
'Moonstone'	7-9
'Unique'	7-8

Blue

	Recommended Zones
'Arthur Bedford'	7-8
'Blue Ensign'	6-8
R. intricatum	6-8
'Blue Jay'	7-8
'Blue Peter'	6-8

Purple

	Recommended Zones
'Anah Kruschke'	6-8
R. catawbiense	5-8
'Daphnoides'	6-8
R. fastigiatum	6-8
'Fastuosum Flore Pleno'	6-8
R. impeditum	6-8
R. keleticum	6-8
'Lee's Dark Purple'	5-8
'Purple Gem'	6-8
'Purple Splendor'	6-8
'Ramapo'	5-8

Rhododendrons by Use

MOST COLD HARDY

White
	Recommended Zones
'Boule de Neige'	5-8
'Catawbiense Album'	5-8
'Dora Amateis'	6-9

Pink
'Caroline'	6-8
'Mrs. Furnival'	6-8
'Parson's Gloriosum'	5-8
'P.J.M.'	5-8
'Scintillation'	6-8
'Windbeam'	5-8

Red
'America'	5-8
'Ignatius Sargent'	5-8
'Nova Zembla'	5-8
'Roseum Elegans'	5-8

Blue
R. intricatum	6-8

Purple
'Anah Kruschke'	6-8
R. fastigiatum	6-8
R. impeditum	6-8
'Lee's Dark Purple'	5-8
'Purple Gem'	6-8
'Ramapo'	5-8

EASY-TO-GROW

White
	Recommended Zones
'Boule de Neige'	5-8
'Dora Amateis'	6-9

Pink
'Anna Rose Whitney'	7-8
R. mucronulatum	5-8
'Pink Pearl'	7-8
'Windbeam'	5-8

Red
'America'	5-8
'The Hon. Jean Marie de Montague'	7-8

Blue and Purple
'Anah Kruschke'	6-8
'Blue Peter'	6-8
'Fastuosum Flore Pleno'	6-8
R. impeditum	6-8
'P.J.M.'	5-8
'Purple Gem'	6-8
'Purple Splendor'	6-8
'Ramapo'	5-8

FULL SUN

White
	Recommended Zones
'Catawbiense Album'	5-8
'Cunningham's White'	6-8
'Dora Amateis'	6-9
'Gomer Waterer'	6-8
R. maximum	5-8

Pink
'English Roseum'	5-8
'Graf Zeppelin'	7-8
'Mrs. Charles E. Pearson'	7-8
'P.J.M.'	5-8

Red
'Nova Zembla'	5-8
'The Hon. Jean Marie de Montague'	7-8
'Vulcan'	7-8

Blue
'Arthur Bedford'	7-8
'Blue Peter'	6-8

Purple
'Anah Kruschke'	6-8
'Daphnoides'	6-8
'Fastuosum Flore Pleno'	6-8
'Purple Gem'	6-8
'Ramapo'	5-8
R. impeditum	6-8

FRAGRANT

White
	Recommended Zones
'Dora Amateis'	6-9
'Fragrantissimum'	9-10
R. moupinense	7-9

Pink
'Caroline'	6-8
R. vaseyi	5-9

Red
'Ignatius Sargent'	5-8

Purple
R. impeditum	6-8

FOR CONTAINERS

White
	Recommended Zones
'Cunningham's White'	6-8
'Dora Amateis'	6-9
R. moupinense	7-9

Pink
'Bow Bells'	7-8
'Mrs. Furnival'	6-8
'P.J.M.'	5-8

Red
'Scarlet Wonder'	6-8

Yellow
'Moonstone'	7-9
R. chryseum	6-7
R. keiskei	7-8
'Unique'	7-8

Purple
R. fastigiatum	6-8
R. impeditum	6-8
R. keleticum	6-8
'Purple Gem'	6-8
'Ramapo'	5-8

DWARF AND SEMIDWARF

White
	Recommended Zones
'Cunningham's White'	6-8
'Dora Amateis'	6-9
R. moupinense	7-9

Pink
'Bric-a-Brac'	8-9
R. pemakoense	7-8
'Windbeam'	5-8

Red
'Carmen'	7-8
'Humming Bird'	7-9
'Scarlet Wonder'	6-8

Yellow
R. chryseum	6-7
R. keiskei	7-8
'Moonstone'	7-9

Blue
R. fastigiatum	6-8
R. impeditum	6-8
R. intricatum	6-8
'Purple Gem'	6-8
'Ramapo'	5-8

THE UNFOLDING OF A RHODODENDRON TRUSS

Rhododendrons produce flowers on branch tips in clusters called trusses. All of the trusses do not open simultaneously, so gardeners can enjoy watching the transition from tightly held bud to fully opened flower truss throughout the blooming season. The various stages of development illustrated in this photographic sequence can take from a week to ten days, depending on climatic conditions. To an avid gardener the gradual unfolding of rhododendron trusses is a natural phenomenon that is a dramatic highpoint of spring.

Rhododendron Societies

The American Rhododendron Society and the Canadian Rhododendron Society are organizations of hobbyists and gardeners with a special interest in these flowering shrubs.

The American Rhododendron Society, founded in 1944 in Portland, Oregon, has 49 chapters and about 5,500 members in the United States and western Canada. It is devoted to encouraging interest in, and knowledge of, rhododendrons and azaleas. It also provides a means for interested people to communicate and cooperate with each other through educational and scientific studies, meetings, publications, and other activities such as rhododendron and azalea shows.

Rhododendrons and azaleas are grown and evaluated in the society's test gardens. Their hardiness and general quality are rated and outstanding new rhododendrons and azaleas are given awards of merit. Published rhododendron ratings are periodically updated. Azalea ratings are now underway.

Membership is open to anyone interested. The annual fee includes the society's publication, *The Quarterly Journal*. Write: The American Rhododendron Society, 14635 S.W. Bull Mt. Road, Tigard, OR 97223.

The Canadian Rhododendron Society was founded in 1971 and includes approximately 400 members. Members are primarily interested in growing and testing plants to select for flower color and plant vigor. Research on plant hardiness is carried out at the Horticultural Research Institute of Ontario at Vineland.

Membership in the CRS includes two glossy bulletins, newsletters, and other materials. Back issues of bulletins are available. There are two annual meetings—one in May or June in conjunction with a flower show, and one in the fall. For information, write Dr. H.G. Hedges, 4271 Lakeshore Road, Burlington, Ontario L7L 1A7.

REPORTS FROM ARS CHAPTERS

A recent poll by the American Rhododendron Society asked its members to detail which azaleas and rhododendrons grew best in their area. A primary purpose of the poll was to benefit new members of the society. Results are especially instructive to any beginner looking for the best and most easily grown varieties and species for a region.

On the following pages are lists of recommended plants from those chapters that responded to the questionnaire. Comments on location, temperatures, prevailing soil type, and other pertinent cultural factors of each chapter area detailed on the following pages make the responses from members of that chapter more meaningful. Responses from each chapter are listed separately for evergreen azaleas, deciduous azaleas, and rhododendrons.

Some chapters provided few or no responses for some of the categories, but this does not mean that categories with few or no responses are unimportant in those areas—often just the reverse is true. As specialists and collectors, the members often responded with those challenging or out-of-the-ordinary plants they have found success with.

For example, the Southeast Chapter mentions only rhododendrons—though this is a world-famous area for evergreen azaleas—because rhododendrons are more tricky there. Similarly, 'Sherwood Red' is omitted by all Northwestern Chapters, though it is a great favorite among the many evergreen azaleas grown there.

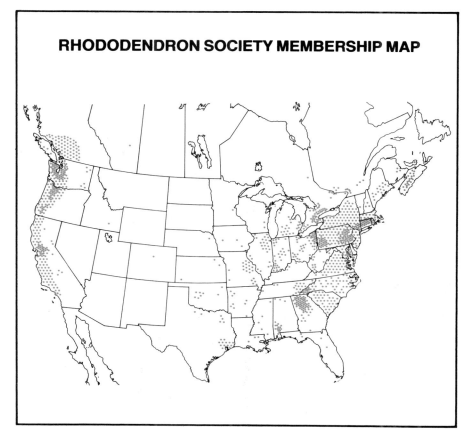

RHODODENDRON SOCIETY MEMBERSHIP MAP

AZALEA CHAPTER

Centered in Atlanta and covering Piedmont and lower Piedmont regions of Georgia. Climate tends to be dry but humid in summer and wet in winter. Summer temperatures reach the 90's or higher. Winter temperature may drop briefly below 0°F. The heavy soil must be lightened and elevated for good, long-term results.

Evergreen azaleas: 'Delaware Valley White', 'Fashion', 'George Lindley Taber', 'Hino-Crimson', 'Pink Pearl', 'Purple Splendor', 'Sherwood Red'.

Deciduous azaleas: *R. atlanticum, R. bakeri, R. canadense, R. periclymenoides, R. vaseyi.*

Rhododendrons: 'Boule de Neige', 'Caroline', 'Dora Amateis', 'Janet Blair', 'Nova Zembla', 'P.J.M.', 'Windbeam'.

CALIFORNIA CHAPTER

Located in the East Bay of the San Francisco Bay Area. Frost seldom occurs, and intense summer heat is seldom experienced because summer climate is modified by fog from the Pacific.

Evergreen azaleas: 'Coral Bells', 'Gumpo', 'Hino-Crimson', 'Hinodegiri', 'Sherwood Orchid', 'Sherwood Red', 'Stewartstonian'.

Deciduous azaleas: 'Cecile', 'Gibraltar', 'Irene Koster', *R. schlippenbachii.*

Rhododendrons: 'Anna Rose Whitney', 'Antoon van Welie', 'Bow Bells', 'Dora Amateis', 'Fragrantissimum', 'The Hon. Jean Marie de Montague'.

CONNECTICUT CHAPTER

Lowest mean monthly temperature varies from 9°F to 34°F, depending on area of the state. Near Long Island Sound the climate is more moderate, seldom experiencing 0°F. In colder areas, snowfall is heavy and long-lasting, protecting plants from wind and low temperatures. Highest mean temperatures vary from 72°F to 78°F over the state.

Evergreen azaleas: 'Delaware Valley White', 'Rosebud', and 'Stewartstonian'.

Deciduous azaleas: 'Gibraltar', *R. arborescens, R. calendulaceum, R. schlippenbachii, R. vaseyi.*

Rhododendrons: 'Boule de Neige', 'Dora Amateis', 'Janet Blair', 'P.J.M.', 'Ramapo', 'Scintillation', 'Windbeam'.

DE ANZA CHAPTER

Located south of the San Mateo Chapter, around San Jose and the Santa Clara Valley. There is occasional frost. Normal winter lows are in the high 30's to mid 40's. Winter highs are 50° to 60°F, and summer highs often in the 90's.

Evergreen azaleas: 'Fielder's White'.

Rhododendrons: 'Anah Kruschke', 'Anna Rose Whitney', 'Antoon van Welie', 'Fragrantissimum', 'The Hon. Jean Marie de Montague'.

GRAYS HARBOR CHAPTER

Located at the base of the Olympic Peninsula on the Pacific Ocean. Soil varies from deep silt loam to clay loam with some gravel benches to sandy loam. Usual temperature extremes are 15°F and 85°F.

Evergreen azaleas: 'Everest', 'Gaiety', 'Gumpo', 'Hino-Crimson', 'Rosebud'.

Deciduous azaleas: 'Cecile', *R. schlippenbachii.*

INDIANA CHAPTER

Located throughout Indiana, where summer high temperatures average 85°F or above. Winter temperature can reach −25°F or lower. Summer is dry. Soil varies from clay to sandy loam to silt loam, slightly acid to neutral in the north and moderately to strongly acid in the south.

Evergreen azaleas: 'Fedora', 'Herbert', 'Stewartstonian'.

Rhododendrons: 'Janet Blair', 'Roseum Elegans', 'Scintillation'.

MIDDLE ATLANTIC CHAPTER

Located in Virginia from the Tidewater to the western mountains. Winter lows may be 15°F at the coast and −5°F near the mountains, with an inverse difference in summer highs. Moderately acid soil is sandy near coast, clay toward the mountains.

Evergreen azaleas: 'Coral Bells', 'Delaware Valley White', 'Herbert', 'Hershey's Red', 'Hino-Crimson', 'Pink Pearl', 'Rosebud', 'Stewartstonian'.

Deciduous azaleas: 'Cecile', 'Gibraltar', 'Klondyke', *R. atlanticum, R. bakeri, R. calendulaceum, R. periclymenoides, R. prinophyllum, R. vaseyi*, 'Toucan'.

Rhododendrons: 'Caroline', 'Janet Blair', 'P.J.M.', 'Roseum Elegans', 'Scintillation', 'The Hon. Jean Marie de Montague'.

MONTEREY BAY CHAPTER

Located mainly in Santa Cruz County, on the coast 75 to 100 miles south of San Francisco. Elevations range from sea level to 2,000 feet. Normal maximum temperature near the coast is 90°F, inland to 105°F, and minimum temperature from 35°F near the coast to 20°F inland. Soil ranges from sand to heavy clay.

Evergreen azaleas: 'Hexe'.

Deciduous azaleas: 'Gibraltar', *R. occidentale.*

NEW YORK CHAPTER

All responses are from Long Island, where temperatures can drop to −10°F and rise to 100°F, but are usually more moderate. Soil varies from sand near shore to clay inland.

Evergreen azaleas: 'Rosebud', Rose Greeley', 'Stewartstonian'.

Deciduous azaleas: 'Gibraltar', 'Klondyke', *R. calendulaceum, R. schlippenbachii, R. vaseyi*, 'Toucan'.

Rhododendrons: 'Boule de Neige', 'Dora Amateis', 'Janet Blair', 'P.J.M.', 'Scintillation', 'The Hon. Jean Marie de Montague', 'Windbeam'.

PIEDMONT CHAPTER

Located in North Carolina, from the Smoky Mountains past the Piedmont and on toward the eastern shore. Temperatures range from 0°F in winter to 100°F in summer. Soil is sandy loam toward coast, clay inland.

Evergreen azaleas: 'Delaware Valley White', 'Pink Pearl'.

Deciduous azaleas: *R. atlanticum, R. calendulaceum, R. periclymenoides*.

Rhododendrons: 'Dora Amateis', 'Roseum Elegans', 'Scintillation', 'The Hon. Jean Marie de Montague'.

POTOMAC VALLEY CHAPTER

Includes northern Virginia, Maryland, southeastern Pennsylvania, and Delaware. Lowest temperature reported was −6°F, but subzero readings are unusual. Summer temperatures are in the 90°F range. Soil near the coast is sandy, but clay is prevalent elsewhere. Drainage can be a problem in clay areas.

Evergreen azaleas: 'Delaware Valley White', 'Rose Greeley', 'Stewartstonian'.

Deciduous azaleas: 'Gibraltar', *R. calendulaceum, R. vaseyi*.

Rhododendrons: 'Caroline', 'Janet Blair', 'P.J.M.', 'Roseum Elegans', 'Scintillation'.

PRINCETON CHAPTER

Located in central New Jersey, extending from "Old Mountains" to seacoast. Low temperatures reach 0°F to −15°F; high temperatures range from 85°F to 105°F. Soil varies from heavy clay to light sand, varying sharply between areas.

Evergreen azaleas: 'Delaware Valley White', 'Hershey's Red', 'Hino-Crimson', 'Rose Greeley', 'Rosebud', 'Stewartstonian'.

Deciduous azaleas: 'Cecile', 'Gibraltar', 'Klondyke', *R. schlippenbachii, R. vaseyi*.

Rhododendrons: 'Janet Blair', 'P.J.M.', 'Roseum Elegans', and 'Windbeam'.

SAN MATEO CHAPTER

Located halfway down the San Francisco Peninsula, which has water on three sides and a low mountain range down the center. Temperatures are seldom below freezing or above 95°F. Soil is mostly clay.

Evergreen azaleas: 'Coral Bells', 'Fielder's White', 'Gumpo'.

Deciduous azaleas: 'Cecile', 'Gibraltar', *R. occidentale, R. schlippenbachii, R. vaseyi*.

SEATTLE CHAPTER

Located in western Washington. There are many microclimates. On the west is Puget Sound, which moderates temperatures near the shore. In the east are two large lakes and, further east, foothills of the Cascades, with elevations up to 1,500 feet. Temperature rarely falls below 10°F or rises above 90°F. Soil is acid.

Deciduous azaleas: *R. schlippenbachii*.

Rhododendrons: 'Bow Bells', 'Dora Amateis', 'Mrs. Furnival', 'The Hon. Jean Marie de Montague', 'Unique'.

SHELTON CHAPTER

Located at the base of the Olympic Peninsula at the southern tip of Puget Sound. Temperature extremes are 0°F and 75°F. Soil is mostly sandy loam but clay occurs in some areas and is acid.

Rhododendrons: 'Anna Rose Whitney', 'Bow Bells', 'Dora Amateis', 'Gomer Waterer', 'Mrs. Furnival', 'The Hon. Jean Marie de Montague', 'Unique', 'Vulcan'.

SOUTHEAST CHAPTER

Located in eastern South Carolina and southern North Carolina. Temperatures range from winter low of 0°F to summer high of 100°F.

Rhododendrons: 'America', 'Blue Peter', 'Boule de Neige', 'Caroline', 'Dora Amateis', 'Janet Blair',

'Mrs. Furnival', 'P.J.M.', 'Ramapo', 'Scintillation', 'The Hon. Jean Marie de Montague'.

SOUTHERN CALIFORNIA CHAPTER

Located over a large area from San Diego to Santa Barbara along the coast and eastward into the mountains to an elevation of 5,000 feet. Soils along the coast are heavy clay, and decomposed granite in the mountains. Summers are dry and hot. Varieties with tolerance to alkaline water are desirable.

Evergreen azaleas: 'Duc de Rohan', 'Gumpo Pink', 'Pride of Dorking', 'Red Poppy', 'Redwings', 'Rosebud', 'Sherwood Red'.

Rhododendrons: 'Anah Kruschke', 'Gomer Waterer', 'Pink Pearl', 'Vulcan'.

TUALATIN VALLEY CHAPTER

Located west of Portland, extending to the Coast Range. Temperature extremes are 10°F and 100°F but do not persist for long periods. Soils vary, but most have excellent drainage and all are acid.

Deciduous azaleas: *R. schlippenbachii*.

Rhododendrons: 'Mrs. Furnival', 'The Hon. Jean Marie de Montague', 'Unique'.

WILLIAM BARTRAM CHAPTER

Located at the juncture of North Carolina, South Carolina, and Georgia. Temperatures range from lows of around −5°F to highs of around 100°F. Soil is predominantly clay loam.

Evergreen azaleas: 'Delaware Valley White', 'Fashion', 'George Lindley Taber', 'Hershey's Red', 'Stewartstonian'.

Deciduous azaleas: *R. bakeri, R. calendulaceum, R. canescens, R. periclymenoides, R. prunifolium*.

Rhododendrons: 'Caroline', 'Dora Amateis', 'Nova Zembla', 'Roseum Elegans', 'Scintillation', 'The Hon. Jean Marie de Montague'.

How to Grow Azaleas and Rhododendrons

Azaleas and rhododendrons have the same basic needs. A well-drained acid soil rich in organic matter is of primary importance. They do even better if a thick mulch covers the soil over their roots, keeping it cool and moist. Some shading from direct hot sun and protection from strong wind is also in order. And they'll do best where summers are cool and humid.

In prime azalea and rhododendron territory—the states along the Atlantic Seaboard and in the Pacific Northwest—it's fairly simple to meet these basic growing requirements. But the more your garden conditions differ from those in these prime areas, the more attention you'll have to give to caring for these shrubs. This chapter covers general care requirements that will be useful wherever you live. If you live outside of prime growing territory, consult pages 20 to 22 for special tips on growing azaleas and rhododendrons in your area.

Whether you are using them in a foundation planting or in a shrubbery border, the planting location must offer azaleas and rhododendrons the proper growing conditions. A good planting site is one where the shrubs look decorative and at home as well as one where proper sun, soil, and moisture are provided.

SUN EXPOSURE

Since they are native to woodlands, most azaleas and rhododendrons grow best with some shade. Deep shade is too dark however, and

At left: Well-cared-for azaleas reward gardeners with a rich display of exquisite floral beauty every spring, year after year.

'Vulcan' rhododendron

'Delaware Valley White' (Glenn Dale Hybrid)

'Anah Kruschke' rhododendron

'Pink Ruffles' (Rutherfordiana Hybrid)

Azaleas planted on the east side of a house receive the half a day of sun that is ideal to promote vigorous healthy growth.

causes plants to bloom poorly. In sunny spots flowers may fade quickly and blooming will be briefer than it would be with more shade. Foliage exposed to hot sun burns and dries out. The tender new leaves that emerge after flowers fade are the most vulnerable to strong sun.

Certain hybrids can stand more sun than others, however. Southern Indica and Brooks Hybrid azaleas, deciduous azalea hybrids, and rhododendrons with small leaves are the most sun-tolerant. In areas with cool humid summers, Pennsylvania for example, deciduous azaleas do well in only light shade. Where there is frequent coastal fog, Oregon for instance, evergreen azaleas and rhododendrons can be planted in full sun. Elsewhere, some shade is needed.

Kinds of shade: Light shade cast by tall high-branching trees is ideal. The tree foliage should diffuse the sunlight, casting constantly shifting shadows, without totally blocking the sunlight. This is the shade found in a woodland garden.

Most home settings cannot provide light dappled shade all day long, but other kinds of shade are also suitable. Planting sites where the shrubs receive half a day of sun are usually satisfactory if the sun is not too hot. This usually means protection from noon sun. Foundation

plantings along the east or west sides of your home will be in half shade.

Assuming that no sides of your home are shaded by trees or other buildings, it's usually best to plant azaleas and rhododendrons along the east side of your home. There they will receive morning sun, which is cooler than the afternoon sun of a western exposure. But if your home is shaded by trees or buildings, this changes the situation. If a western exposure is lightly shaded in both summer and winter, it is a perfectly fine planting spot. Shaded southern exposures will also do, but shade must be provided year-round throughout at least the hottest part of the day.

Planting beds along northern sides of buildings receive no direct sunlight. They may be too dark for best growth and flowering, however if the bed is open to the sky and unshaded by trees, enough light is often reflected onto the shrubs to support good growth. White walls or a nearby fence can reflect light and increase the brightness.

Shrub borders or planting areas on flat land away from the shade of your house should be shaded by overhead trees or located in the shadow cast by fences or evergreen windbreaks. Half a day of shade is usually sufficient and, as with shrubs shaded by a house, morning sun is usually best.

On sloping ground and hillsides, azaleas and rhododendrons do best on slopes facing east or west. Southern exposures are usually too hot and dry, while northern ones are too cold. Shade from trees and protection from wind can of course alter the conditions and make unfavorable exposures more acceptable.

Sun and cold: During winter when temperatures are below freezing, some of the water in living plant tissues is actually frozen. Chemical changes within a dormant plant allow it to be unharmed by this frozen state, as long as freezing and thawing of the tissue is gradual. In areas where winters are very cold, dormant flower buds can be damaged when struck by early morning sunlight because the buds thaw too rapidly. Protection from the earliest morning sun is advisable in such situations.

WIND PROTECTION

In any climate, wind can damage rhododendrons and azaleas. Cold winter winds can severely dehydrate plants, as can hot dry summer wind in arid climates. Wind can also tear the large evergreen leaves of rhododendrons. Blossoms of both rhododendrons and azaleas can be tattered or even blown off.

Avoid planting these shrubs near windy corners of your house or in narrow areas where winter winds funnel between buildings. In open areas, wind can be slowed down with a windbreak of tall evergreens or a fence. Both hedges and fences should not stop wind completely, or the wind will be swept directly over the top, resulting in damaging turbulence on the other side. Fences and hedges with small gaps allow wind to pass through at a slower, safer velocity.

COLD SPOTS

Cold air, like water, flows downhill and collects in "puddles." On windless nights, it collects at the bottom of a slope, and in this cold spot frost will occur before it forms anywhere else in your garden. Other frosty spots where cold air collects are places where the downward flow of cold air is stopped—for instance, along a solid fence or hedge halfway down a hillside. Don't plant on the uphill side of such a barrier. (See pages 60 and 63 for more information on protecting plants from cold.)

SOIL

Soil on a forest floor is usually highly organic, composed of decaying leaves, twigs, stems, bark, and fallen plants. Such soil is at the same time both moist and well-aerated. The decaying plant parts hold large quantities of water, but because they are only partially decomposed they are held together loosely, leaving generous air pockets. As the plant material decays, nutrients and organic acids are released, creating a rich, acidic soil. The annual autumn leaf fall adds to the natural compost and renews the soil.

Azaleas and rhododendrons have very fine, shallow root systems. Because this soil is so loose, rich, and moist, the roots don't have to work very hard pushing through it.

Most garden soil is a far cry from forest soil. In most gardens however, with very little soil modification azaleas and rhododendrons can do well. Azaleas will do well in a rich garden loam as long as it is properly acidic. Sandy loams are ideal, since they offer both richness and aeration. But soil that is too sandy, has a high clay content, or is alkaline will have to be improved.

Improving clay and sand: Soil texture is the key to preparing a good soil for azaleas and rhododendrons. Clay soil has a dense texture, draining slowly and admitting very little air, which is necessary for healthy root growth. Sand has too loose a texture, with so many air spaces that water drains through it too quickly. It holds little in the way of moisture and nutrients. The structure of both sandy and clay soils is improved by adding organic matter. This breaks up clay so that the resulting soil is more crumbly, holding more air and allowing water to drain more quickly. Sandy soil is made denser and more water-retentive.

Both of these soil types need generous quantities of organic matter such as peat moss, leaf mold, compost, or composted ground bark. Perlite could also be added to soil that has a very high clay content. Spread 3 to 8 inches of organic matter on top of the soil, and spade it in to depth of 1-1/2 to 2 feet, depending upon how much the soil needs to be improved. For a large planting of azaleas and rhododendrons, you can use a power tiller to work the entire planting bed. For just a few shrubs, add organic matter in a 2- to 3-foot radius of where the shrub's trunk will be. (See planting instructions on page 56.)

The organic matter will make the soil more acidic. This is useful in maintaining acidity in acid soil and necessary in soil that is not acidic enough for azaleas and rhododendrons. In alkaline soil, more drastic steps have to be taken. (See following section on soil pH.)

Wet spots: Even where soil texture offers good drainage, waterlogging may be a problem in some spots in your garden. Do not plant azaleas and rhododendrons in low spots of your property where water collects after a rain. Such waterlogged soil is certain death for most kinds—only an unusual water-tolerant species such as the swamp azalea, *R. viscosum*, could grow in such a site. Sloping sites where water drains quickly are best, especially if soil tends to be heavy.

If your garden has a drainage problem that can't be corrected, you can get around it by planting in raised beds, mounds, or in containers. (See page 55 for more information.)

Soil pH: Azaleas and rhododendrons prefer an acid soil with a pH between 4.5 and 5.5. A measure of acidity or alkalinity, pH is read on a scale of 1 to 14, with the lower numbers being most acidic and the higher numbers most alkaline. The midpoint, 7, is neutral. Most plants prefer a slightly acid pH of 6.5. Azaleas and rhododendrons can only absorb certain necessary nutrients, iron and manganese for instance, through their roots when these nutrients are in the chemical forms found in acid soil.

Soil pH varies throughout the continent, ranging from acidic on the East and Northwest Coasts to alkaline in arid regions of the Midwest and Southwest. In areas where rainfall is high, pH tends to be acidic, because the rain washes the alkaline elements calcium and magnesium from the soil. Where soils are high in organic matter, this also contributes to soil acidity. Forests and woodland areas tend to have more acidic soil, though the type of bedrock will influence this. Areas with limestone bedrock will have a higher pH.

You can determine the pH of your garden's soil by using a test kit available at most garden centers. Test each area where you are growing, or intend to grow, azaleas or rhododendrons, since the pH can vary from place to place in your garden. The soil along your house foundation may be more alkaline because lime in the cement foundation leaches into the surrounding soil. Soil tests are also available from private companies and usually from your local county agricultural extension agent.

A sylvan setting with light filtering through tree branches most closely approximates the native growth conditions of azaleas and rhododendrons.

You can lower your soil's pH by adding ground agricultural-grade powdered sulfur. It is slow-acting and should be applied several months in advance. Yearly applications may be needed if irrigation water washes alkaline elements back in.

The amount of sulfur to add depends upon your initial soil pH and how much you want to lower it. The more alkaline the pH, the more sulfur will be needed to lower it 1 point. To change the pH from 6.5 to 5.5, work 1-1/2 pounds of sulfur per every 100 square feet into the soil. Use 1/3 more in clay soil and 1/3 less in sandy soil. The following table gives other amounts for different situations.

Lowering pH	Amount of sulfur per 100 sq ft		
Change in pH	Sandy	Loamy	Clayey
8.5 to 6.5	4 lb	5 lb	6 lb
7.5 to 6.5	1 lb	1½ lb	2 lb
7.5 to 5.5	2 lb	3 lb	4 lb
6.5 to 5.5	1 lb	1½ lb	2 lb

Applying acidifying fertilizers such as iron sulfate and ammonium sulfate, especially in areas where soil acidity is borderline, will help maintain the appropriate pH. (See page 58 for more about fertilizers.) And a gradually decomposing organic mulch will also help keep the soil acid. (See page 58.)

A GOOD START

For the fullest enjoyment of your azaleas and rhododendrons, it's important to get them off to a good start. And that good start begins at the nursery by selecting the healthiest shrubs. If you take care of them before planting, plant them properly and in the right conditions, and coddle them a bit for the first year, they'll be off to a very good start.

Plant selection: Shrubs for sale at the nursery are available either as container-grown or as balled-and-burlapped plants. Shrubs in metal, plastic, or fiber containers were grown in those containers and their entire root system is intact. Balled-and-burlapped shrubs were grown in the ground and recently dug up. Their ball of roots and soil is wrapped up in protective burlap. Because they were dug from the field, they have lost some roots and are more fragile than container-grown shrubs.

After you bring the shrubs home, keep them in a cool shaded spot until planting time. If left in the sun, dark containers can heat up quickly to root-damaging temperatures and burlapped rootballs will quickly dry out. Balled-and-burlapped shrubs should be planted as soon as possible so transplanting shock is minimized. Container plants can be kept for several weeks as long as they are watered regularly and kept cool.

Choose sturdy well-branched plants with thick foliage. Weak spindly ones probably have underdeveloped root systems and will transplant poorly, perhaps never gaining full vigor. Older, larger plants have more woody tissue and are hardier than smaller plants, a significant advantage where winters are severe.

HELP WHERE SOIL IS ALL WRONG—RAISED BEDS, CONTAINERS, AND MOUNDS

In the Southwest, soil is too alkaline for azaleas and rhododendrons and cannot be amended successfully. In parts of Southern California and the Deep South, soil has a high clay content and drains slowly, encouraging root rot. In these unlikely areas, it is still possible to grow fine azaleas and rhododendrons. The secret is to plant above ground in an ideal soil mix.

For individual plants, grow them in large decorative containers such as redwood pots or cement planters. For shrub borders or foundation plantings, soil can be held in raised beds that resemble large planter boxes, or piled on top of the ground in large mounds.

Soil: You can use any commercially available planting mix that's high in organic matter such as peat. Many people prefer to mix their own, however. The Southern California Chapter of the Rhododendron Society recommends a mix containing equal parts coarse peat moss, ground fir bark, and coarse perlite.

Raised beds: Build raised beds from railroad ties, wood, brick, unmortared or mortared stone, whatever fits in with the architecture of your home. Be aware that the cement in concrete and mortar is highly alkaline and can change the pH of your soil mix. If wood is used, be sure it is rot-resistant such as redwood or cedar.

Beds should be at least 1-1/2 to 2 feet deep and 3 feet wide. If the underlying soil drains slowly, lay down 2 inches of coarse gravel before adding the soil mix. Provide drainage holes along the bottom of all sides of the raised beds.

Mounds: For a less structured look than raised beds create, you can pile soil mix on top of the bad soil in natural-looking mounds. Make the mounds at least 2 feet deep and gradually slope them towards the natural grade of the land. Gravel should be used beneath the mound if the underlying soil is slow-draining. Erosion may be a problem on newly built mounds unless they are very wide. Mounds are useful in creating woodland gardens where soil conditions are unfavorable. Locate mounds well away from tree trunks. If you place too much soil over tree roots they will smother.

Containers: Tubs and planters have the special advantage of being movable. In areas of extreme cold, you can plant in containers and bring the plants indoors to a bright, but cool, place for the coldest months. Or if container plants are borderline hardy, you can simply move the container to a spot protected from direct winter sun and wind. But be aware that the soil in containers will be colder than soil in the ground.

Be sure containers are large enough for the plant, since soil dries rapidly in containers. Because azaleas and rhododendrons have shallow roots, width is more important than depth—roots may not grow to the bottom of deep pots. Planters should have drainage holes and are best watered until water runs from the holes. Be sure to water even in winter if the soil is dry.

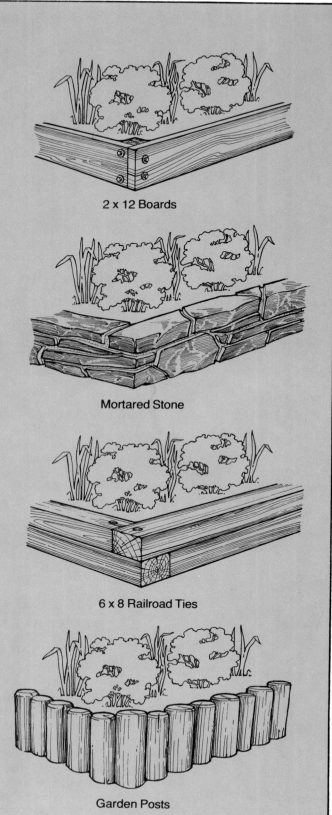

2 x 12 Boards

Mortared Stone

6 x 8 Railroad Ties

Garden Posts

In a mass planting, space young plants far enough apart so that their branch tips will just touch or lightly intermingle when they have reached mature size. 'Delaware Valley White' (Glenn Dale Hybrid) pictured above.

Choose the largest plants that fit your budget, but don't be fooled by mere size. The shrub's top growth should be in proportion to its roots. The root system of an overly large container-grown plant is crowded and coiled and transplants poorly. A balled-and-burlapped shrub with a large top and a small rootball has lost too many roots and cannot adequately supply the top growth with water.

When to plant: Azaleas and rhododendrons can be planted in spring when they are in flower. This timing allows you to choose pleasing colors and simplifies arranging color combinations in your garden. Spring is the best time for planting in areas with cold winters because it allows the shrub time to get established before winter. Summer is harder on azaleas and rhododendrons than winter, so fall planting is recommended in areas where soil doesn't freeze at all, or only for short periods. Summer planting is hazardous in any climate, but can be done safely if plants are kept well-watered and given extra attention.

The planting hole: A planting hole dug much bigger than the rootball and filled back in with improved soil will give a shrub the best start. This will provide the roots with soil that is a gradual transition between the soil it was grown in and your garden's soil. Roots will be able to penetrate the soil easily and plants will become established more quickly.

A hole about 1-1/2 times as deep and as wide as the rootball is usually recommended. Dig out the soil and place it on a tarpaulin or sheet of plastic. Mix in organic matter such as moist peat moss or compost. If your soil is very sandy or very heavy clay, you may have to take more drastic measures. (See page 55.) Use this amended soil as backfill to refill the hole.

First refill the bottom of the hole with backfill so that the shrub will be sitting at the proper level—with its rootball about an inch above ground level to allow for settling. Fill the planting hole part way with water to settle the backfill. Allow the water to drain, then position the plant in the hole with the most attractive side facing forward.

A container-grown shrub can be removed from its can by grasping its trunk and gently twisting and pulling. The rootball should come out all in one piece if it is properly moist. Though some people advocate it, if a plant is grown in a fiber container it is better not to plant the container along with the plant. By the time the container has rotted, the shrub's roots will be growing in a tight circular pattern and will not grow outward as they should.

The burlap surrounding a balled-and-burlapped rootball can be planted along with the plant. Unfasten the burlap and fold it back, laying it along the bottom of the planting hole after the plant is in position. The burlap will eventually rot. Do not remove it before planting, or the soil may fall away from the roots.

A balled-and-burlapped plant may have roots encased in particularly heavy clay soil from the growing field. If you place such a rootball into desirably crumbly, well-draining soil, the clay will block water and nutrients from being absorbed by the rootball. Water and fertilizer

Soil

Clay soil has smooth texture and retains moisture.

Sandy soil is gritty, loose, and fast-draining.

Loam soil combines the best features of clay and sandy soils.

Planting

Prepare a planting hole 1-1/2 times width and depth of plant rootball. Place soil removed on a tarp.

Amend soil removed from planting hole with organic matter. Place a small amount of amended soil into planting hole.

Add water to planting hole to wet and settle backfill soil.

Raise or lower rootball until its top is 1 to 2 inches higher than surrounding soil.

Add backfill to hole surrounding rootball. Firm with hands and add water twice before completely filling hole with backfill.

Use remaining backfill to form a water-holding basin over the outer edge of the rootball. Water thoroughly.

will flow past the rootball but won't be absorbed. If a shrub you are planting has a heavy clay rootball, remove all or most of the clay soil with a gentle stream of water from a hose and then plant immediately.

After the plant is positioned, fill around the rootball with backfill, firming with your hands as you go. Water thoroughly to settle soil around the rootball and to eliminate any air pockets. This is best accomplished in two steps. First fill the hole halfway with backfill then water thoroughly. Firm the soil in place with your hands. Then add the remaining backfill, water, and firm soil again. Be sure the rootball is slightly above soil level—if it is too deep the surface roots may suffocate. A water basin made of a ring of firmed soil directly over the edge of the rootball will help catch water, allowing it to soak into the rootball.

Spacing plants: Ideally, shrubs should be spaced so that they will not be crowded at maturity. When full-grown, their branch tips should touch or intermingle slightly if planted in a foundation planting or in a shrub border. In woodland gardens or in an Oriental garden, shrubs should have spaces between them for a more natural look.

Since most azaleas grow to a 4- to 6-foot diameter and large rhododendrons grow even bigger, they should be spaced about 5 feet apart from trunk to trunk, depending upon the ultimate size of the plant. Place the trunk about 2-1/2 to 3 feet from a fence or wall.

Most people tend to plant closer than this, since new shrubs planted so far apart look skimpy. But if planted too close, the shrubs will quickly become crowded and jumbled looking. One way to avoid the problem is to space small plants about 2-1/2 feet apart and after they begin to look crowded in 3 or 4 years, transplant every other shrub to another spot in the garden.

Transplanting: Since azaleas and rhododendrons are shallow-rooted, they transplant very easily. Even fairly large plants can be moved if they are dug with as large a rootball as possible. This is best done in early spring in cold-winter climates and in fall in climates with mild winters and hot summers. If many roots are lost during transplanting, or if you are moving large mature shrubs, cut back a proportionate amount of top growth.

ROUTINE CARE

When grown under proper light and soil conditions in an amenable climate, azaleas and rhododendrons need very little care. Providing for their basic needs is simple once you know how.

Watering: Newly transplanted shrubs are particularly vulnerable to drying out because their roots are shallow. During the first growing season, water plants slowly and thoroughly, keeping the soil moist but not soggy. Check to be sure the water is soaking into the rootball.

When in bloom and during growth in spring, azaleas and rhododendrons need plenty of water. Drought during blooming results in short-lived flowers. If water is lacking during spring and early summer, new growth will be stunted and flower buds for the next season's bloom will be sparse.

During periods of summer drought, water shrubs weekly. Water can be tapered off in late summer, since this encourages dormancy and preparation for winter. However, shrubs should not go into winter lacking water because once soil freezes roots cannot take up water, and cold wind and winter sun dehydrate plants. (See page 21.) If autumn rains do not provide adequate water, give plants a thorough watering after the first fall frost.

Mulching: In their native habitats, azaleas and rhododendrons grow with a layer of fallen leaves forming a natural mulch over their roots. They will thrive in your garden if you provide them with a similar mulch that keeps the soil moist and their roots cool. These shrubs have very delicate roots that can be damaged by extremes of temperature and water supply, and even by shallow hoeing. A mulch prevents rapid changes in soil temperature and slows moisture loss, while shading out competitive weeds.

A wide variety of organic materials are suitable for use around azaleas and rhododendrons. A thick covering of fallen autumn leaves or pine needles is easy to come by in many gardens.

If the quantity of fallen leaves isn't sufficient, many types of agricultural by-products can make effective and good-looking mulches. Some of these may only be available locally. Grape pomace (spent grape seeds and stems), bagasse (spent sugar cane), and peanut hulls are economical. Ground composted fir bark is very attractive though more expensive. Shredded leaves are both effective and attractive.

Spread the mulch over the soil beneath and somewhat beyond the spread of the branches to a depth of about 2 inches. A mulch of fallen leaves should be deeper since they will pack down once wet. Renew in spring and fall as needed.

The importance of a mulch cannot be overemphasized. Though shrubs may seem to do well without it, they will decline over a period of years. An organic mulch slowly decays, and as it does it adds nutrients to the soil, while maintaining the soil's loose, water-retentive texture and acid condition.

Fertilizing: Experts disagree about whether azaleas and rhododendrons need to be fertilized. If grown in a rich loam and covered with a thick, organic mulch, they probably do not need extra nutrients by way of fertilizer. But since most garden soils aren't ideal, most experts advise light applications of fertilizer.

Use fertilizer designed for azaleas, rhododendrons and camellias, sometimes labelled RAC, or one designed for acid-loving plants. It's best if nitrogen is in the form of urea or ammonium sulfate rather than nitrate compounds. Potassium sulfate is preferred over potassium chloride.

Rake back the mulch and sprinkle the fertilizer on top of the soil under the branch spread of each shrub. Carefully follow the package directions as to the

Watering

Apply water slowly so that it soaks through mulch and into soil without runoff.

Several kinds of sprinklers work efficiently and are a convenient way to apply water. The spray washes and cools leaves.

A soaker hose applies water efficiently at a rate soil can absorb, directly over rootball.

Mulching

A 2- to 3-inch layer of non-compressing pine needles is a long-lasting, attractive, acid mulch.

Fallen leaves make a good mulch. The mulch layer should be deeper than other mulches as leaves pack down when wet.

A mulch of fir bark is long-lasting and attractive. It is widely available and helps maintain proper pH and moisture.

Fertilizing

Granular fertilizer is most beneficial when applied directly on top of soil under mulch.

Bury long-lasting fertilizer pellets, 2 or 3 inches below soil and beyond the outer edges of the rootball.

Foliar fertilizers (especially chelated iron) are conveniently applied using a hose-end sprayer.

amount of fertilizer to use. Mature shrubs usually need between 1/8 and 1/4 pound of 10-10-10 (10% nitrogen, 10% phosphorus, and 10% potassium).

Fertilizer can be applied once in spring or more lightly once a month until midsummer. Fertilizer applied after midsummer will stimulate undesirable tender growth that may be injured by frost in fall. Some experts apply a fertilizer containing no nitrogen (0-10-10) in late summer or fall—this does not stimulate growth and is thought to increase cold tolerance.

Azaleas or rhododendrons grown in pots or tubs need regular fertilizer. Slow-release kinds can be mixed in with the soil and are effective over long periods of time. Light applications of liquid fertilizers applied with weekly waterings from spring through summer are also good.

Avoid repeated or excessive use of superphosphate or high phosphorus fertilizers. Phosphorus might lock up soil iron and cause chlorosis. It is best to apply phosphorus fertilizers if their use is indicated by a soil test.

Winter protection: Cold temperatures alone can kill or injure azaleas and rhododendrons, but very cold sunny days, hot winter sun reflected off snow, and cold drying winds are further culprits. (See page 21 for more information.) The best protection against winter damage is selecting azaleas and rhododendrons that are completely hardy in your climate. But since young plants are more susceptible to desiccation from cold wind and winter sun, in harsh climates you may wish to give them some protection during their first winter.

You can protect plants by erecting a windbreak around them. (See illustrations on page 63.) A simple windbreak can be made from burlap and wooden stakes. Surround individual plants with this shelter; it will also shade them from direct sun. Anti-desiccant sprays, available at your garden center, can also be sprayed on evergreen foliage to provide a protective waxy coating.

PRUNING

You may wish to prune azaleas and rhododendrons to control their size and shape, to encourage a fuller, more dense plant, and to rejuvenate old, overgrown, or lanky shrubs. But in many cases, if given enough room to grow in the first place, very little pruning will be needed. In most gardens, these shrubs' natural shapes are the most attractive.

Pruning azaleas: To promote dense growth, pinch off the tips of new growth, approximately half an inch, in spring or early summer after flowering and before the stems have hardened. This will cause side branches to form, creating a denser, fuller plant, with a natural shape.

To shape a plant that is growing too large for its allotted space, you can cut into the shrub and prune out carefully chosen branches to thin the shrub. Use one-handed clippers and cut off the branches where they emerge from larger branches. Then to reduce size, clip back the ends of the remaining long branches. These cuts can be made anywhere along a branch, since azaleas form growth buds along the whole length of their branches. For a graceful natural shape, let the branching pattern tell you where to make the cuts.

For formal-looking azaleas, you can clip shrubs in spring with hedge shears. Be sure to prune very soon after flowering or you will cut off the following year's flower buds, which form by midsummer. Shearing too late in the season results in odd-looking shrubs with polka-dotted groups of flowers and leaves.

Large, leggy overgrown azaleas can be cut back severely to rejuvenate them. Using heavy shears or a saw if necessary, cut back all main branches to about a foot from the ground. This must be done in late winter or early spring so new growth can mature by fall. Provide generous fertilizer and moisture during this period of regrowth.

Pruning rhododendrons: Unlike azaleas, rhododendrons do not produce growth buds along their stems. Dormant buds are largely confined to the leaf axils. Cuts must be made with more care.

Naturally compact or well-branched rhododendrons do not need pruning. But those that by nature are leggy with few branches can be encouraged towards bushiness. Pinch off the new growth in spring as it is elongating from the bud. This will cause dormant buds from lower down on the stems to grow into branches, making a fuller plant.

Tall, rangy, or overgrown rhododendrons can be rejuvenated by cutting them back drastically. Cut back the stems in early spring or late winter to about 2 feet long. Study the stems and try to locate marks where leaves once were attached. Dormant buds are buried there beneath the bark. It may take as long as 6 to 8 weeks for new growth to sprout.

Some experts recommend cutting back rhododendrons over a period of three years, cutting only a third of the stems each year. This is less of a shock to the plant, but means the rejuvenation process will take longer.

Dead-heading: Faded flower clusters should be removed from rhododendrons and from deciduous azaleas. This is called dead-heading. Removing the old clusters improves the plant's appearance. It also improves the plant's vigor because it prevents energy from being wasted on seed formation. Dead-heading is best done immediately after flowers fade. You can simply press the base of a flower cluster between thumb and forefinger and snap if off. Be careful not to injure the nearby buds.

Problems and Solutions

As with any shrub, azaleas and rhododendrons are occasionally bothered by insects or disease. The type of problem varies from region to region and with weather conditions. The following pests are the most common ones—from time to time others may be troublesome. A knowledgeable nurseryman or your county agricultural extension agent can advise you further on diagnosis and treatment.

Pruning

Remove spent rhododendron blossoms, being careful of nearby growth buds.

Pinch rhododendron shoot tips in late spring to keep plant dense and bushy, and to increase the number of flowering shoots.

Occasional removal of the oldest rhododendron branches will rejuvenate leggy, overgrown plants.

Pinch azalea shoot tips after flowering to maintain plant shape and force more flowering branches to grow.

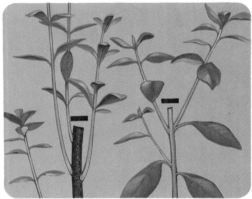

Cut branches of healthy, established azaleas at any point and vigorous, upright growth from many latent buds results.

Remove dead branches and vertical branches that destroy azalea plant symmetry at their origin.

Problems and Solutions

Nursery specialists familiar with local conditions and potential plant problems are an excellent source of advice.

Leaves chewed by black vine weevil are not attractive, but more serious damage is caused by larvae working below soil level.

When a pest problem requires chemical treatment read and follow product labels carefully and spray thoroughly.

Lace bug: The azalea lace bug can be severe on azaleas and rhododendrons. Tiny nymphs (immature insects) and mature fly-like insects, which are 1/8 inch long with lacy wings, feed on the undersides of the leaves, sucking the sap. The damage is unsightly and the plant's vigor is reduced by heavy infestations.

Damage first appears in spring. On rhododendrons small white specks or blotches appear on the upper sides of the leaves. The undersides of azalea leaves develop rusty-colored varnish-like spots. Several generations of lace bugs can be produced during each growing season, developing into a serious problem as the season progresses.

Lace bugs are most troublesome in the East and South and on plants grown in full sun. Providing shade will reduce infestations. Sprays of carbaryl, malathion, Ficam®, or Metasystox-R® will control insects. Apply as soon as symptoms are noticed; repeat in several weeks. Be sure to wet leaf undersides.

Whiteflies, mealybugs, spider mites: These are only occasional pests. Hose down plants with a stream of water to remove insects, or use an insecticidal soap since the soap won't harm beneficial insects. If the problem persists, use insecticides such as Kelthane® for mites and Orthene® for mealybugs and whiteflies.

Black vine weevil: This serious pest of rhododendrons sometimes troubles azaleas and is serious on other plants including yew and hemlock. The blackish-brown beetle measures 3/8 of an inch long and has a hard shell and no wings. Beetles live in the soil at the bases of the plants and emerge at night to feed on the leaves, chewing characteristic semi-circular notches along the leaf margins.

The worst damage is done by the larvae, which feed on the roots. These small white, curved grubs destroy the fine root hairs and may also strip the stem of bark. Damage from the larvae causes the plant to wilt even when the soil is moist. If you pull the soil away from the plant's crown, you may be able to observe the root damage.

Larvae feed on roots in early spring, then pupate and emerge as beetles in early summer. Adult beetles feed on leaves for about a month, then lay eggs that soon hatch into larvae. Larvae feed before hibernating for the winter.

Control beetles with two applications of Orthene® or Ficam®. Spray when beetle damage is first observed and then in 2 or 3 weeks to kill later-emerging beetles. Spray both the ground around and under the plant and the lower leaves and branches.

You may also try to control beetles without insecticides. Lay boards on the soil beneath the plant at night. The beetles feed on the leaves while it is dark and will hide under the boards when it is light. Turn over the boards each morning and collect the beetles and any larvae.

DISEASES

Root rot: Rhododendrons and azaleas can suffer from root rot, caused by the widespread fungus *Phytophthora cinnamoni* during warm wet summers if they are grown in slowly draining soil. Roots and then stems rot. The first observable symptom is wilted yellowing leaves that hang onto the plant. The plant may die soon after wilting is first noticed. If you cut into the stem of a plant that has root rot, you will notice reddish streaks under the bark caused by the fungus.

Root rot is difficult to cure because once symptoms are noticed it's too late to apply fungicide. The best prevention is to plant shrubs in well-aerated, fast-draining soil. If rhododendrons and azaleas die of root rot, do not replant in the same spot without first improving soil drainage.

Petal blight: This devastating fungus disease can wipe out azalea flowers seemingly overnight. (Rhododendrons may also be affected.) The fungus starts as tiny white pinpricks on the petals (brown spots on white flowers), and by the next day the blossoms are reduced to a slimy mass. The blight is serious in the South and occurs in other eastern areas where high humidity and warm days encourage the fungus.

Petal blight is spread by rain splashing the fungus spores from the soil onto the plants. Cleaning up any blighted petals and not allowing them to drop to the ground will help control the disease. In areas where the blight is severe, it is necessary to drench the soil with terrachlor or Turban® before blooming and to spray the flowers with Thiram® or Zineb®. Use a fine spray mist. Apply the fungicide three times a week beginning when the buds show color. The blight is worse on mid- and late-season azaleas, since spores are not active when early azaleas bloom.

CULTURAL PROBLEMS

Salt injury: If too much fertilizer is applied to azaleas and rhododendrons, or if irrigation water is high in salt, the shrubs' fine roots may be damaged. Damaged roots cannot take up water, and leaves will brown on the edges or all over, depending upon the severity of the problem. Older leaves may show symptoms first. These symptoms also appear on underwatered plants, frequently those grown in tubs or pots.

If salt injury is due to fertilizer, water heavily several times to leach salts away from roots. When watering container plants, be sure water runs out drainage holes each time it's watered.

Iron chlorosis: If the soil pH is over 6 (see page 53), azalea and rhododendron roots cannot absorb necessary nutrients, especially iron. Iron-deficient leaves become chlorotic (lack green chlorophyll) and appear yellow with distinct green veins.

Chelated iron, available at your nursery, applied to the soil and sprayed on the leaves as a foliar fertilizer, will help plants to become green. Repeat several times during the growing season. You should also take steps to lower the soil pH, but chelated iron will bring immediate help.

WINTER PROTECTION

Some of the rhododendrons and deciduous azaleas are among the most hardy of all flowering shrubs. Still, methods of shielding plants from drying winter winds or bright winter sun are important: Perhaps you are interested in testing the northern limit of a hardy evergreen azalea such as one of the Kaempferi Hybrids. Also, young plants are never as hardy as older, more established plants. Winter protection is advisable for a young plant's first two winters in your garden if hardiness is even slightly marginal.

Here are some techniques of winter protection that have proved useful for many azalea and rhododendron gardeners.

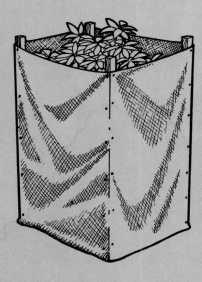

Fence the plant with burlap attached to stakes set far enough away from plant so burlap does not touch shrub.

Shield plant from sun and wind with a frame of plywood held in place with stakes.

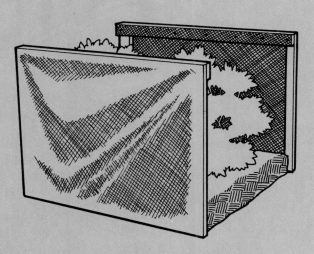

Burlap fastened to wooden frames used on one or two sides of plant protect it from sun damage. (Fill with leaf mulch if needed.)

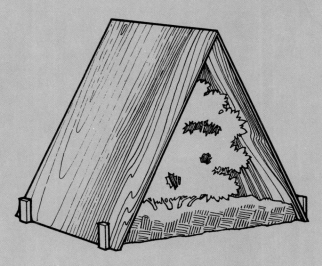

Plywood A-frame gives good protection and keeps snow sliding off a roof from damaging plant.

Index

Photographs indicated by bold numbers.